Cause & Effect: The Fall of the Soviet Union

Hal Marcovitz

ReferencePoint
Press®

San Diego, CA

About the Author

Hal Marcovitz is a former newspaper reporter and columnist. A resident of Chalfont, Pennsylvania, he is the author of more than 170 books for young readers.

© 2016 ReferencePoint Press, Inc.
Printed in the United States

For more information, contact:
ReferencePoint Press, Inc.
PO Box 27779
San Diego, CA 92198
www. ReferencePointPress.com

LIBRARY OF CONGRESS CATALOGING-IN-PUBLICATION DATA

Marcovitz, Hal.
  Cause & effect: The fall of the Soviet Union / by Hal Marcovitz.
    pages cm. -- (Cause & effect in history)
  Audience: Grades 9 to 12.
  Includes bibliographical references and index.
  ISBN-13: 978-1-60152-792-9 (hardback)
  ISBN-10: ISBN 1-60152-792-6 (hardback)
 1. Soviet Union--Politics and government--1953-1985--Juvenile literature. 2. Soviet Union--Politics and government--1985-1991--Juvenile literature. 3. Soviet Union--Economic policy--Juvenile literature. 4. Soviet Union--Military policy--Juvenile literature. I. Title. II. Title: Fall of the Soviet Union. III. Title: Cause and effect: The fall of the Soviet Union.
  DK277.M37 2016
  947.085'4--dc23
                                                                    2014048804

CONTENTS

"History is a complex study of the many causes that have influenced happenings of the past and the complicated effects of those varied causes."

—William & Mary School of Education,
Center for Gifted Education

Understanding the causes and effects of historical events is rarely simple. The fall of Rome, for instance, had many causes. The onslaught of barbarians from the north, the weakening of Rome's economic and military foundations, and internal disunity are often cited as contributing to Rome's collapse. Yet even when historians generally agree on a primary cause (in this instance, the barbarian invasions) leading to a specific outcome (that is, Rome's fall), they also agree that other conditions at the time influenced the course of those events. Under different conditions, the effect might have been something else altogether.

The value of analyzing cause and effect in history, therefore, is not necessarily to identify a single cause for a singular event. The real value lies in gaining a greater understanding of history as a whole and being able to recognize the many factors that give shape and direction to historic events. As outlined by the National Center for History in the Schools at the University of California–Los Angeles, these factors include "the importance of the individual in history . . . the influence of ideas, human interests, and beliefs; and . . . the role of chance, the accidental and the irrational."

ReferencePoint's Cause & Effect in History series examines major historic events by focusing on specific causes and consequences. For instance, in *Cause & Effect: The French Revolution*, a chapter explores how inequality led to the revolution. And in *Cause & Effect: The American Revolution*, one chapter delves into this question: "How did assistance from France help the American cause?" Every book in the series includes thoughtful discussion of questions like these—supported by facts, examples, and a mix of fully documented primary and secondary source quotes. Each title also includes an overview of the event so that readers have a broad context for understanding the more detailed discussions of specific causes and their effects.

The value of such study is not limited to the classroom; it can also be applied to many areas of contemporary life. The ability to analyze and interpret history's causes and consequences is a form of critical thinking. Critical thinking is crucial in many professions, ranging from law enforcement to science. Critical thinking is also essential for developing an educated citizenry that fully understands the rights and obligations of living in a free society. The ability to sift through and analyze complex processes and events and identify their possible outcomes enables people in that society to make important decisions.

The *Cause & Effect in History* series has two primary goals. One is to help students think more critically about history and develop a true understanding of its complexities. The other is to help build a foundation for those students to become fully participating members of the society in which they live.

IMPORTANT EVENTS IN THE HISTORY OF THE SOVIET UNION

1848
Karl Marx and Friedrich Engels publish *The Communist Manifesto*, providing the intellectual timber for the Communist revolution in Russia and establishment of a classless society.

1939
Stalin and Nazi dictator Adolf Hitler sign a nonaggression pact, enabling the Soviet Union to occupy countries in Eastern Europe. Hitler soon turns against Stalin and invades the USSR.

1927
Joseph Stalin seizes power in Russia on his way to becoming one of the world's most ruthless dictators.

1914
World War I erupts when Austria-Hungary attacks Serbia; Russia enters the conflict to protect the Slavic citizens of Serbia.

1850 — 1910 — 1920 — 1930 — 1940

1928
To revive the Soviet economy, Stalin institutes his Five-Year Plan, which collectivizes Soviet farms and nationalizes Soviet industries. Nevertheless, the Soviet Union drifts into famine.

1903
Vladimir Lenin ascends to the leadership of a radical Communist movement in Russia known as Bolshevism.

1921
The civil war ends when the Communist, or Red, forces prevail.

1917
After three years of battlefield losses and strife at home, Czar Nicholas II is forced to abdicate; a shaky democratic government in Russia is quickly overthrown by Lenin and the Bolsheviks. A month after the Bolshevik takeover, civil war breaks out in Russia.

1905
On January 9, Russian troops fire into a crowd of labor activists, killing two hundred. The massacre, known as Bloody Sunday, becomes a symbol of the injustices suffered by Russian workers.

6

1945
World War II ends; American, British, and Soviet leaders carve up Europe, placing much of Eastern Europe under Soviet dominion.

1962
The Soviets attempt to establish a nuclear missile base in Cuba; for thirteen days the United States and USSR teeter on the brink of war, until Soviet leader Nikita Khrushchev backs down and removes the missiles.

1988
Fighting breaks out in the autonomous region of Nagorno-Karabakh in Azerbaijan between Muslim Azeris and Christian Armenians; the fighting has continued into the 2010 decade.

1949
The Soviet Union conducts its first successful test of an atomic weapon.

1991
Hard-line Communists stage a coup against Gorbachev; the coup collapses when the army refuses to support the hard-liners. The failed coup sparks the breakup of the Soviet Union.

1950   **1965**   **1980**   **1995**   **2010**

1980
Ronald Reagan wins the US presidency and makes it clear he considers the Soviet Union a threat to world peace; Reagan commences an arms buildup that costs tens of billions of dollars.

2010
Civil war erupts in Kyrgyzstan as Kyrgyz insurgents attack ethnic Uzbeks.

1985
Mikhail Gorbachev ascends to the leadership of the Soviet Union and enacts a series of economic and human rights reforms designed to boost his country's low standard of living.

2014
Russia invades Ukraine as part of a campaign to block Ukrainian trade with the West.

End of the Cold War

For decades, the Union of Soviet Socialist Republics—commonly known as the USSR or Soviet Union—stood firm as one of the world's superpowers. It was a nation with a huge and diverse population, an abundance of natural resources, fearsome military might, and a stockpile of nuclear weapons. But the people of the Soviet Union, and the peoples of the countries aligned with the Soviets, lived under totalitarian governments and economies based on the principles of socialism and communism. Under socialism, all property in a society is owned and shared equally by the people. Communism takes this philosophy a step forward, advocating government control of all industry, agriculture, and other private property. Moreover, Communists believe the state should use violent means, if necessary, to seize factories and farms from private ownership.

Following World War II the Soviet Union and the United States maintained a competition to spread their influences to the various corners of the planet. This was the era of the Cold War. It was not an actual armed conflict between the two superpowers, but rather an often devious competition in which both countries attempted to maintain influence over the peoples of Europe, Africa, the Middle East, South America, and Asia. Mostly, the Cold War was fought by spies and spy satellites, as well as by bomber pilots, submarine skippers, and missile silo commanders—all of whom awaited orders to launch nuclear weapons at the enemy.

Proxy Wars

If Soviet and American troops had ever directly faced each other, it is possible the conflict would have escalated beyond the use of conventional weapons and ultimately resulted in the launch of nuclear warfare. President Ronald Reagan, who served in the White House from 1981 to 1989, recalled his reaction when learning that in the event of a nuclear attack on the United States, he would have a mere six minutes to make a decision to launch a counterattack against the USSR. "For the first time in history, man had the power to destroy mankind itself," Reagan said. "A war between the superpowers would incinerate much of the world and leave what was left of it uninhabitable forever."[1]

Although Soviet troops never directly faced American troops in combat, there were occasional proxy wars. These involved conflicts in which each side faced enemy soldiers armed with weapons and aided by advisors and intelligence provided by the opposing superpower. By engaging in these proxy wars, both sides sought to exert their influence in strategically important corners of the globe without actually confronting one another—and risking nuclear war.

During the 1960s the Vietnam War was one such proxy war as the North Vietnamese soldiers and Vietcong guerrillas, armed with weapons provided by the USSR, battled American troops and their South Vietnamese allies. Similarly, the 1979 invasion of Afghanistan by Soviet troops turned into a proxy war as well. In that war Soviet soldiers fought Afghan guerrillas armed with weapons supplied by the US Central Intelligence Agency.

> "For the first time in history, man had the power to destroy mankind itself. A war between the superpowers would incinerate much of the world and leave what was left of it uninhabitable forever."[1]
>
> —US president Ronald Reagan.

Coup Against Gorbachev

But all wars eventually end, and in 1991 the Cold War came to an abrupt close when members of a hard-line faction in the Politburo—the policy-making wing of the Soviet Communist Party—attempted to stage a coup against Soviet president Mikhail Gorbachev. To Gorbachev and other reformers, it was abundantly clear that the economic principles of communism and the institutionalized totalitarianism of Soviet culture were leading the USSR on a path to destruction. Indeed, the concept of communism—first enunciated some 150 years earlier—held that all working people should share in the common wealth of the state. In practice, though, the people living under communism invariably found themselves enduring lifetimes of meager wages.

And so Gorbachev instituted a series of reforms in which he hoped to guide the Soviet Union on a path toward a market-based economy in which his country could open trade with the industrialized nations of the West. Dissident movements in many Soviet bloc countries had broken out as well. Protesters demanded human rights, self-determination, and democracy—qualities of life they were denied under Soviet rule. Gorbachev realized the human rights movements could not be stifled with shows of force by the Soviet military—which had often been the USSR's response to similar protests in the past. So his reforms included granting measures of freedom to the peoples of the Communist bloc.

Hard-liners bristled under Gorbachev's reforms, fearing that his administration would destroy a political system in which they still fervently believed. On August 19, 1991, as Gorbachev vacationed at a summer home, eight top officials in the Politburo dispatched troops to arrest the Soviet leader. Meanwhile, army tanks were mobilized and

Tanks and buses form a roadblock outside the Russian White House, which houses the country's parliament, during a 1991 coup attempt. Lacking public and military support, the coup attempt failed. This event marked the Soviet Union's final days.

ordered to roll into the USSR capital of Moscow as a show of force illustrating that a new regime had taken power. The plotters, led by vice president Gennady I. Yanayev, issued a terse statement claiming they had arrested Gorbachev and seized power because "a mortal danger had come to loom large."[2]

Displays of Heroism

The Soviet people responded to this show of force not with sheepish acceptance but with displays of heroism. In Moscow, Boris Yeltsin, who had recently been elected president of the Russian Soviet Socialist Republic—the largest state within the Soviet Union—hopped aboard a tank and faced down the approaching soldiers. Surrounded by thousands of pro-democracy demonstrators, Yeltsin called on the Soviet military to lay down its arms. "Soldiers, officers, generals," he declared, "the clouds of terror and dictatorship are gathering over the whole country. They must not be allowed to bring eternal night."[3]

Yeltsin's plea found traction among the soldiers he faced. Many did lay down their weapons, and the tanks turned back. When the Soviet army refused to support the coup, the insurrection collapsed. Gorbachev was released and returned to Moscow.

> "The clouds of terror and dictatorship are gathering over the whole country. They must not be allowed to bring eternal night."[3]
>
> —Boris Yeltsin, president of the Russian Soviet Socialist Republic.

But as the coup collapsed, so did the Soviet Union. By turning against the coup leaders, the Soviet people declared they would no longer endure communism, totalitarianism, or the way of life they had known as pawns in the Cold War. Empowered by his national celebrity in defying the hard-line Communists, Yeltsin led the breakup of the Soviet Union. That winter, the fifteen Soviet Socialist Republics declared their independence. Moreover, the former Soviet bloc countries declared their freedom as well; they embraced democracy, free-market economics, and human rights as fundamental components of their national characters.

A Brief History of the Soviet Union's Collapse

The founding of the USSR can be traced to a slim book written in 1848 by two German journalists: Karl Marx and Friedrich Engels. At the time Marx and Engels drafted their treatise, *The Communist Manifesto*, Europe was undergoing a transition. For hundreds of years, virtually all wealth in Europe was concentrated in the hands of the titled aristocracy: nobles who inherited their wealth, particularly vast tracts of land. To ensure the wealth of Europe remained within this small aristocratic society, the sons and daughters of the aristocracy never married outside their circle.

The wealthiest and most powerful members of this society were the kings and queens who ruled over their countries. There were frequent wars between countries, but none of these wars resulted in the spoils of victory shared with the peasantry. Invariably, peasants remained peasants regardless of who sat on the throne.

When Marx and Engels published their manifesto, many countries in Europe were moving away from societies dominated by aristocrats to forms of democracy in which citizens had a say in the direction of their governments. For the most part, authority in Europe was still wielded by powerful rulers, but many of them agreed to rule with the participation of elected parliaments.

Moreover, Europe was also transitioning from an agrarian society to an industrial society. With the invention of motorized power—through steam engines as well as petroleum-driven engines—mass production was now possible. Factories were built throughout Europe, providing employment to millions. Industrialization brought great wealth to factory owners, but the lives of those who toiled on the assembly lines were no better off than those of the peasants who labored on the farms of the landed gentry. Pay was low, working hours were long, and the work could be dangerous. Injuries and deaths were common occurrences on factory floors.

According to Marx and Engels, the history of the world could be defined in terms of the struggle between these two classes of people. The rich owners of land or factories used their wealth and influence to exploit working people. It was time, Marx and Engels declared, for workers to rise up and seize control of human civilization, establishing a classless society—a society where wealth was shared equally by all. "Workingmen of all countries unite!"[4] declared the authors.

Lenin Joins the Bolsheviks

Nowhere did these words resonate more loudly than in Russia, where the aristocracy controlled virtually all the country's wealth while peasants and factory workers toiled for near-slave wages. By the 1880s the work of Marx and Engels prompted college student Vladimir Ulyanov to immerse himself in the plight of the workers. Due to his radicalism on campus, Ulyanov fell under constant watch by authorities under the command of the

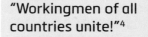

"Workingmen of all countries unite!"[4]

—Karl Marx and Friedrich Engels, authors of *The Communist Manifesto*.

Russian monarch, Czar Alexander III. Ulyanov also found inspiration in another book by Marx, *Das Kapital* (*Capital*). Marx declared in the book that the primary motivation of the industrialist is to accumulate capital, or money, and the method in which this goal is accomplished is the exploitation of the workers. Says British journalist and author Ronald Clark, "*Das Kapital* . . . revealed to him the external world. . . . It was certainly in this period that he began to master the book and use it as a tool."[5]

Ulyanov obtained a law degree in 1892. Making his home in the city of Samara, Ulyanov represented peasants in disputes against wealthy merchants and landowners. As he saw the harsh treatment meted out to his clients, Ulyanov convinced himself of the righteousness of a classless society. Under communism, there are no aristocrats and no peasants—only citizens who live on equal terms.

Ulyanov joined subversive organizations intent on overthrowing the czar. In 1895 Ulyanov and other Marxists were arrested. He was sentenced to serve three years in a labor camp in Siberia—the harsh and frigid region of Russia near the Arctic Circle.

A banner in Moscow's Red Square in the 1980s depicts the three men who were instrumental in the founding of the Soviet Union and its Communist system: Vladimir Lenin, Friedrich Engels and Karl Marx..

Following his release, Ulyanov settled first in Munich, Germany, then returned to Russia, making his home in St. Petersburg, where he took a leadership role in the Communist movement. He also took a new name—Vladimir Lenin—to avoid the scrutiny of the czar's police, who knew Vladimir Ulyanov to be a dangerous subversive worth watching. Lenin was by no means a moderate—he had no taste for negotiating with the czar to win better terms for working people. Instead, he wanted nothing less than a takeover of the Russian government. At a 1903 meeting of Russia's Social Democratic Labour Party, Lenin declared, "Give us an organization of revolutionaries and we will overturn Russia!"[6] It was at this meeting that Lenin ascended to the leadership of the most radical wing of the party. Lenin's group was known as the Bolsheviks—in English, the Majority.

Fall of the Kerensky Government

More than a decade would pass before the Bolsheviks truly represented a majority of Russians. The events leading to the Bolshevik takeover commenced in 1914 when Russia waged war against Germany in a conflict that soon enveloped the entire European continent. On one side stood the armies of Germany, Austria-Hungary, and Turkey, then known as the Ottoman Empire; they were opposed by Russia as well as the Allied Western European democracies, mainly Great Britain and France, although in the last year of the conflict the United States joined the Allied cause. The Great War, later to be known as World War I, took a heavy toll on Russia. During Russia's three-year involvement in the war, the czar—by now Nicholas II—mobilized an army of 12 million men; by 1917 more than 9 million Russian soldiers had been killed, wounded, or taken prisoner. As Russia's fortunes in the war deteriorated, the Russian people grew less patriotic about the conflict than they had been at the outset. Too many husbands, brothers, and sons were dying or sustaining horrific wounds on the battlefield. And too many people back home were subsisting on little food and enduring freezing temperatures with hardly any coal to heat their homes.

German ruler Kaiser Wilhelm II was a canny leader who saw an opportunity to force Russia out of the war. With Russia no longer a threat, Wilhelm planned to transfer his troops to the Western Front to engage the French and British, against whom the Germans had been locked in a stalemate since 1914.

"Give us an organization of revolutionaries and we will overturn Russia!"[6]

—Bolshevik leader Vladimir Lenin.

In April 1917 the kaiser sent a train to Switzerland to retrieve Lenin, who had been living there in exile since 1914. Knowing that the rabble-rousing Communist leader would stir dissent against the Russian government, Wilhelm transported Lenin to St. Petersburg. By now the czar had abdicated, and the Russian government was under the shaky control of a democratically elected prime minister, Alexander Kerensky. In October 1917 Lenin led a coup against the Kerensky government—which fell with little resistance. Now the head of the Russian government, Lenin negotiated a treaty with Wilhelm, who could now withdraw troops from the Eastern Front. (This maneuver by the Kaiser did not lead to a German victory. Bolstered by American troops, in 1918 the Allies pushed the Germans back, forcing a German surrender and an end to the war.)

Birth of the USSR

Lenin, meanwhile, had his own war on his hands. A month after the Bolsheviks seized power, anti-Communists still loyal to the czar or the Kerensky government banded together and waged war against the Communists. The so-called White forces fought against the Communists, or Reds, for three years.

By 1921 the Reds had prevailed. Their opponents lacked the resolve or the military prowess of the Communists. After declaring victory, the Bolshevik government wrote a constitution, and on December 29, 1922, Communist leaders from Russia as well as the neighboring states of Ukraine, Byelorussia, and Transcaucasia adopted a treaty creating the Union of Soviet Socialist Republics. Over the next two decades, the USSR moved aggressively to absorb its neighbors, and by 1940 the country consisted of fifteen Soviet Socialist Republics.

Lenin did not live to see the USSR blossom into a powerful nation. He suffered strokes in May 1922 and March 1923. Near the end of his life, Lenin expressed dismay at the direction of the new country. Soviet citizens were still mired in poverty, and the economy had yet to recover from the war years under the czar as well as the havoc of the civil war. Moreover, Lenin had grown alarmed that one of his top aides, Joseph Stalin, was amassing widespread powers. He feared Stalin aimed to make himself into a dictator.

Lenin died in 1924. And, as Lenin feared, Stalin made a grab for power. His chief opponent was Leon Trotsky, a longtime Lenin ally. Stalin proved himself a much better politician and by 1927 forged many alliances on the Central Committee—the body of Communist Party leaders who held power in the Soviet Union. Stalin ordered Trotsky expelled from the Central Committee and in 1929 exiled him from the Soviet Union. In 1940 Stalin sent an assassin to kill Trotsky. The killer, finding Trotsky living in Mexico, murdered Stalin's nemesis with an ax.

Stalin's Paranoia

Such brutality was common under Stalin, who emerged as one of the world's most autocratic and vindictive dictators. During the 1930s Stalin ordered a series of purges to eliminate political opposition. The

purges may have sent as many as 20 million Soviet citizens to their deaths or slave labor camps in Siberia.

Stalin's paranoia was driven by several factors. He knew his country was economically weak, and efforts to modernize industry or farming lagged behind other European nations. Stalin was also aware that Germany, his country's chief antagonist, was rearming following its defeat in World War I. Germany was now under the leadership of Nazi dictator Adolf Hitler, who maintained a deep hatred for communism. Hitler also believed the Slavic people of Russia and other European countries were racially inferior to the Germans of northern European descent—known as Aryans—and made no secret of his desire to dominate the Slavic countries. "The Slavs are a mass of born slaves, who feel the need of a master," Hitler said in September 1941, in notes dictated to a secretary. "Our role in Russia will be analogous to that of England

Fate of the Czar

One sad chapter of Russia's civil war involved the fate of the former czar, Nicholas II, and his family. After the czar's abdication in March 1917, the government led by prime minister Alexander Kerensky was unsure of what to do with the former monarch. Nicholas, his wife, and five children were held under house arrest at a palace in St. Petersburg.

The czar and his family lived in comfort for several months, but after the Bolshevik takeover they were granted few freedoms. Many Communist leaders demanded the czar be put on trial. The Bolsheviks transferred the family to a house in Ekaterinburg, a city in the Ural Mountains just north of the Russian border with Kazakhstan. Soon White forces besieged the city. Bolshevik leaders feared the Whites would reach the czar and free him, providing anti-Communists with a spiritual victory as well as a leader with a hard resolve to wipe out the Reds.

Near midnight on July 17, 1918, guards at the Ekaterinburg home received a telegram from Bolshevik leader Yakov Sverdlov ordering the executions of Nicholas and his family. The family was hastily awoken and told to dress—guards told them they were being moved to a new city. As Nicholas and his family prepared to leave the home, they were ushered into the basement along with four of their loyal servants. The guards opened fire and within seconds the last czar of Russia, along with all members of his family and their unfortunate servants, were shot to death.

in India [as conquerors]. . . . To-day everybody is dreaming of a world peace conference. For my part I prefer to wage war for another ten years rather than be cheated of the spoils of victory. . . . The German people will raise itself to the level of this empire."[7]

Hitler, in fact, had designs on conquering Europe—including the Soviet Union. But he was also savvy enough to know that he could not win a two-front war: Fighting the French and British on the Western Front while facing the Soviets on the Eastern Front. And so he made peace overtures toward Stalin, which the wily Soviet dictator was happy to accept. Stalin had his own designs on dominating Eastern Europe.

On August 23, 1939, German and Soviet diplomats signed the Nazi-Soviet Pact, a treaty that divided several Eastern European countries between the two powers—among them Poland, Romania, and Lithuania. A week after signing the nonaggression pact, German troops invaded Poland, igniting World War II. When Germany attacked the Poles, Stalin moved Soviet troops into eastern Poland, laying claim to the territory and placing it under the dominion of the Soviet Union.

The Iron Curtain

Hitler and Stalin did not stay allies for long. Hitler had always intended to invade the Soviet Union, and on June 22, 1941, the German army launched Operation Barbarossa: the invasion of the USSR. At first, the German army pushed far into the Soviet Union, coming within 40 miles (64 km) of Moscow. But the Soviet army dug in, and by early December the German advance stalled. The Soviets were aided by the harsh Russian winter, in which temperatures plunged as low as -40°F (-40°C). The Soviet army launched a massive counterattack, and by mid-December the Germans were in retreat.

America entered the war in December 1941 following the Japanese attack on Pearl Harbor, Hawaii. By May 1945 the German army was defeated, and the leaders of the United States, Great Britain, and the Soviet Union held summits to determine the future of Europe. From these summits, a divided Europe was forged, with most of the countries in the East under the dominion of the Soviet Union. This was the beginning of the Cold War, in which Stalin and his successors aimed to spread communism and Soviet domination while the Western democracies initiated a foreign policy designed to stem the spread of Soviet influence. The Cold War was also punctuated by the development of nuclear weapons, as each side amassed an arsenal of devastating bombs capable of ending life on the planet.

Meanwhile, in Europe, the "Iron Curtain" was established—a term first used by British prime minister Winston Churchill in 1946—separating the Soviet-dominated countries from the free democracies

"The Slavs are a mass of born slaves, who feel the need of a master. Our role in Russia will be analogous to that of England in India [as conquerors]."[7]

—Nazi dictator Adolf Hitler.

of Europe. The Iron Curtain was not a physical wall; still, the borders were heavily policed with the intent of stifling emigration from the Soviet bloc states to the democracies of Western Europe.

Stalin died in 1953. He was succeeded by Nikita Khrushchev, who sought to expand Soviet influence beyond the Iron Curtain. His most daring gambit occurred in 1962 when Khrushchev convinced Fidel Castro, the Communist leader of Cuba, to permit the Soviets to base nuclear missiles on the island—just 90 miles (145 km) from Florida. The scheme was discovered by US Air Force spy planes, which photographed the missile base under construction. President John F. Kennedy demanded the Soviets remove the missiles. At first Khrushchev refused, and for ten days in October 1962, the United States and Soviet Union teetered on the brink of nuclear war. Khrushchev ultimately backed down and removed the missiles.

Long Lines at the Market

The Soviets continued their efforts to spread their influence beyond Eastern Europe. During the 1960s and 1970s, countries such as Cuba, Nicaragua, Vietnam, Egypt, and Angola could count on financial aid and weapons supplied by the Soviets. But there were missteps in Soviet foreign policy. In December 1979 the Soviet Union invaded Afghanistan, touching off a ten-year conflict between Soviet soldiers and Afghan guerrilla fighters (whose arms were supplied by the Central Intelligence Agency). The Soviets found themselves in a long and relentless conflict and finally, in 1989, withdrew their forces.

By then the economy of the Soviet Union was near collapse. Much of the industrialized West refused to trade with the Soviets. This denied the Soviet Union trading partners who would otherwise be willing to purchase Soviet goods and, especially, the country's oil. As a result, consumer goods were often in short supply in Soviet cities. Long lines in front of shops and grocery stores were common scenes on the streets of Moscow and other cities.

Moreover, Soviet citizens bristled under the heavy hand of the state government, which denied them many basic human rights. These restrictions dated back to the Stalin era and had been kept in place by subsequent Soviet regimes to ensure government control over all aspects of life in the USSR and in the Soviet-dominated countries.

Moscow residents crowd into a state-owned shop in 1991 in hopes of buying meat. The shop received a rare shipment of meat from Western Europe.

In the Soviet Union the most feared agency of government was the KGB, the *Komitet Gosudarstvennoy Bezopasnosti* (Committee for State Security). The KGB was a spy network that kept close watch over all subversive elements of Soviet society.

But even the KGB could not stifle democratic revolutions that were underway in the Soviet bloc countries—especially in Poland, where an organized labor movement known as Solidarity gained widespread support among the Poles. By now the Soviet head of state was Mikhail Gorbachev, who realized the dire state of his country's economy as well as the futility of trying to maintain iron-fisted control over the restive peoples of Soviet bloc nations. Gorbachev made overtures to improve relations with the West—albeit under the dictates of a Communist regime.

Winston Churchill, prime minister of Great Britain during the World War II era, first used the term *Iron Curtain* to describe the domain of the Soviet Union. "From Stettin in the Baltic to Trieste in the Adriatic an iron curtain has descended across the Continent," Churchill said during a 1946 speech. "Behind that line lie all the capitals of the ancient states of Central and Eastern Europe. Warsaw, Berlin, Prague, Vienna, Budapest, Belgrade, Bucharest and Sofia; all these famous cities and the populations around them lie in what I must call the Soviet sphere."

As Churchill said, the Soviets exerted their will over many neighboring countries. Among the countries whose leaders took their orders from Moscow were Poland, Romania, Bulgaria, Czechoslovakia, Hungary, and East Germany. (Germany was divided by the Allies at the end of World War II; West Germany, a democracy, was aligned with the West, its government supported by America and the Western European democracies.)

Moreover, following the creation of the Soviet Union in 1922, Soviet leaders used their military to invade neighboring nations and absorb them into the USSR—making them into Soviet Socialist Republics. By 1940 the USSR included the following Soviet Socialist Republics: Russia, Ukraine, Belarus, Estonia, Georgia, Latvia, Lithuania, Moldova, Tajikistan, Kazakhstan, Uzbekistan, Azerbaijan, Armenia, Turkmenistan, and Kyrgyzstan. The territory of the USSR represented one-sixth of the earth's landmass—some 8.5 million square miles (22 million sq. km).

Quoted in Paul Halsall, "Winston S. Churchill: 'Iron Curtain Speech,' March 5, 1946," Fordham University Modern History Sourcebook, 1997. www.fordham.edu.

A Nation out of Step

But by 1991 the Soviet economy had fallen too far into a tailspin. By then several Soviet bloc countries had severed their ties with the USSR and installed democratic governments. Elsewhere, rioting broke out across the Soviet domain, forcing Gorbachev to send troops to Soviet Socialist Republics such as Kazakhstan, Armenia, Georgia, and Uzbekistan. By late 1991 the Soviet Union had all but crumbled. The final blow occurred when Russian president Boris Yeltsin declared independence from the Soviet Union. Under Yeltsin, Russia established a democracy, eliminated the Stalin-era police state, and opened trade with the West. On December 8, 1991, the Soviet Union ceased to exist.

The USSR lasted just sixty-nine years. During that time, the country grew into a superpower, able to challenge the United States in terms of military strength and international influence. But the principles on which the Soviet Union was built—totalitarian government, state control of all aspects of life, a classless society—ultimately remained out of step with what people would tolerate in their governments or how nations could prosper.

CHAPTER TWO

How Did Czarist Policies Contribute to the Rise of Communism?

Discussion Questions

1. Do you think the Bolsheviks would have won over the Russian people if the czar had taken steps to improve the lives of average citizens? Explain your answer.
2. Could Nicholas have done anything to prevent the bloodshed that took place during the Bloody Sunday demonstration, and would it have made any difference? Explain your answer.
3. Do you think Nicholas could have kept his throne if Russia had waged a more successful war against the Germans? Why or why not?

By the time czar Nicholas II ascended the throne of Russia in 1894, members of his family—the Romanovs—had ruled Russia for about 280 years. Nicholas became czar—or emperor—of Russia during a period in which many European countries had accepted democracy. Some countries, among them Great Britain and France, were governed by legislatures elected by their citizens. Others, such as Germany, were ruled by constitutional monarchs: The head of state was still a monarch, who inherited the throne through the death of a parent or other close relative, but an elected legislature also had a voice in the government, making laws and guiding the decisions of the king or queen.

But that was not the case in Russia. By the end of the nineteenth century, Russia was still firmly entrenched as an empire where the czar ruled with autocratic authority. Says journalist and historian Richard

Charques, "For the peasantry the czar was indeed the anointed ruler. Supreme judge and lawgiver, raised above all the appointed 'estates' of the realm, he was the father of his people who felt for them as a father should."[8] Russians of the era lived by an expression: *Do Boga vysoka, a do czaria daleko*—meaning, "Heaven is high and the czar is far off."

On the map, Russia is a huge nation. East to west, the country spans some 6,200 miles (9,978 km) from the shores of the Bering Sea, just 55 miles (89 km) from Alaska, to its western border with Finland. The northernmost portion of Russia lies above the Arctic Circle. In the south the country's border runs through the Caucasus Mountains—gateway to the deserts of the Middle East. For centuries, the wealth of this land, rich in agriculture, minerals, and other natural resources, remained firmly in the hands of high-born aristocrats. When Nicholas II took power, the population of Russia was some 130 million people—and most of them were mired in relentless poverty.

Russia's Industrial Revolution

Among Russia's poor was Georgi Gapon, the son of a Russian peasant, who was born in 1870 in the city of Poltava. In 1902 he entered the priesthood of the Russian Orthodox Church and became a hero among Russia's destitute. In 1903 Gapon founded the Assembly of Russian Workers—one of the first trade unions in Russian society. The wealthy factory owners vehemently opposed trade unions, believing they would lead to higher wages for workers. At the time, Russia was undergoing an industrial revolution, thanks to the efforts of two of the czar's finance ministers: Ivan Vyshnegradsky, who served from 1887 to 1892, and his successor, Count Sergei Witte.

> "We ourselves shall not eat but we shall export."[9]
>
> —Ivan Vyshnegradsky, finance minister to the czar.

Vyshnegradsky and Witte both insisted that for the Russian economy to grow, the people would have to make sacrifices. Vyshnegradsky once said, "We ourselves shall not eat but we shall export."[9]

Vyshnegradsky and Witte oversaw expansion of the country's railroads and believed strongly in enlarging Russia's industrial base. To enrich the Russian economy, they encouraged Russian factories to export their goods. Crops were exported as well. To encourage farmers to export their crops, Vyshnegradsky and Witte convinced Nicholas to impose heavy taxes on farmers who raised their prices. It meant foreign buyers could purchase Russian-grown grains at cheap prices. Such a policy also insured there would be less food available for the Russian people.

Under Czar Nicholas II (pictured in a painting from 1900) Russia made great strides in building factories and developing industry, but factory workers and peasants toiling in the fields did not share in the nation's wealth.

By 1904 Russia had made great strides in building factories and developing its industrial strength as well as becoming a supplier of food for other countries. But the workers in the factories and peasants in the fields did not share in Russia's wealth. Most farmers owned very small plots of land that did not enable them to make much of a profit on their crops. Instead, much of Russia's agricultural land was still owned by the Russian aristocracy. Moreover, 1904 was a particularly bad year for Russia's farmers. Due to the harsh Russian winters, the country's growing season is normally quite short. The winter of 1904 was even colder than usual with icy weather lasting into the spring months, delaying the planting season and leading to a poor harvest that fall.

Labor Strikes and Warfare

Russian factory workers were no better off than the workers in the farm fields. Russia's industrialists were loath to share their profits with the lowly workers who labored on the assembly lines. Crammed into tiny and unsanitary apartments in Russia's cities, workers seethed over their low pay, long hours, and modest living conditions. Occasionally, labor strikes erupted in the cities: In 1896 and 1897 a labor strike in St. Petersburg virtually shut down the city's textile industry.

Such strikes were illegal because, in the czarist Russia of the late nineteenth and early twentieth centuries, labor unions were illegal. Russian authorities, however, seemed unsure of what to do about the strikes. The czar, under pressure from the aristocracy and the country's industrialists, resisted demands by workers for higher pay or to legalize their labor unions. Many advisors to the czar urged Nicholas to crush the unions, but Witte advised Nicholas to take a moderate approach. Witte feared wider unrest should the czar begin a harsh campaign to crack down on unions.

As 1905 arrived, Nicholas found himself embroiled in problems far from home. In 1904 Russia went to war with Japan over control of trade in the Chinese region of Manchuria. Mostly fought at sea, the Russo-Japanese War inflicted a heavy toll on the Russian navy, which suffered devastating defeat. In 1905 Nicholas was forced to withdraw Russian troops from Manchuria, giving up the territory to the Japanese.

As Nicholas's attention was drawn to the war in Manchuria, the life of the Russian worker remained dismal. In many Russian cities—particularly St. Petersburg—riots erupted as hungry people demanded food. The poor Russian harvest of the previous fall meant that whatever food was available was prohibitively expensive to the average Russian family. In December 1904 a strike by twelve thousand workers at the Putilov machinery company quickly spread to other factories in St. Petersburg, with more than one hundred thousand workers throwing down their tools and staying off their jobs.

March on the Palace

That month Gapon started meeting with workers in St. Petersburg, planning a public demonstration to show workers' discontent. It was decided that Gapon's group, the Assembly of Russian Workers, would lead a march through the streets of St. Petersburg, ending at the steps of the Winter Palace—the luxurious wintertime residence of the czar and his family. Upon arrival at the palace, leaders of Gapon's group planned to ask for a meeting with the czar in which they would petition for higher wages, lower food prices, and more rights, including a voice in the government. The petition read:

> Sire! We the workers, our children, families and defenceless aged parents, have come to you to seek justice and protection. We are in deepest poverty and oppressed with labours beyond our strength. We are treated like slaves who must suffer in silence. . . . Despotism and arbitrary rule are suffocating us. Sire, our strength is exhausted and our patience has run out. Things have become so terrible for us that we would prefer death to the unbearable torment we are being forced to suffer.[10]

During a meeting of the assembly, one labor leader rose from his seat and asked, "And what, comrades, if the Ruler will not receive us and does not want to read our petition?" From those assembled came the shouts of: "Then we have no Czar!"[11]

Mutiny Aboard the Battleship *Potemkin*

One of the most dramatic events of the 1905 revolution was the mutiny aboard the battleship *Potemkin,* whose crew seethed under the discipline of cruel officers. On June 27, while cruising in the Black Sea, the men complained when the ship's cook served a meal riddled with worms. An officer responded by shooting a crewman. A melee ensued and the officer was tossed overboard. Many of the seven hundred crew members then armed themselves, shot the other officers, and seized the ship.

The *Potemkin* docked briefly in the Ukrainian port of Odessa to stage a funeral for a slain mutineer; while the ship was in port, the government learned of the mutiny. The *Potemkin* put to sea again to search for a friendly port to take on supplies and fuel. The mutineers hoped to restock and rearm the *Potemkin* and employ the ship as a weapon in the uprising against the czar. Meanwhile, the czar dispatched ships to sink the *Potemkin.* When the ships drew within firing distance, gunners defied orders, refusing to fire on fellow sailors. Rather than risk mutinies aboard their ships, the captains turned about and headed for their home ports.

Finally, the *Potemkin* limped into the Romanian city of Constanta, where crew members surrendered. Romanian officials permitted most to remain in their country. About sixty returned to Russia, where they were tried for treason. Seven crew members, regarded as ringleaders, were sentenced to death; the remaining defendants served lengthy prison terms.

Bloody Sunday

Word of the demonstration spread throughout St. Petersburg. On January 9, 1905—a Sunday—Gapon led a march of some twenty thousand workers through the streets of the city. Although they intended to present the czar with a list of demands, the workers did not want to appear as antagonists. Gapon counseled the marchers to remain peaceful. Many carried placards displaying the czar's portrait. They also joined in patriotic songs, including the hymn "God Save the Czar." Among many Russians, the czar was still a revered figure known as the "Little Father."

Demonstrators cry out as hundreds of dead and wounded lie in the snow after soldiers fired into a crowd seeking a meeting with the czar on January 9, 1905. The day came to be known as Bloody Sunday.

Unknown to the demonstrators, the czar was not even in the palace. News of the protest had reached the czar's ministers, who advised him to refuse to meet the marchers and, in fact, stay away from the palace. Instead, when the marchers arrived at the palace, they found themselves facing hundreds of nervous soldiers.

Suddenly, a shot was fired. The first blast was followed by hundreds of others as soldiers fired into the crowd. Within minutes, some two hundred demonstrators lay dead in the snow. Another eight hundred sustained wounds. Watching from the Winter Palace, Witte reported what he saw:

From my balcony, I could see a large crowd moving along. . . .
It contained many women and children. Before ten minutes

had passed, shots resounded in the direction of the Troitsky Bridge. . . . A bullet whizzed past my head, another one killed the porter of the Alexander Lyceum [hotel], I saw a number of wounded being carried away from the scene in cabs, and then a crowd running in disorder, with crying women here and there. . . . The troops fired without rhyme or reason. There were hundreds of casualties . . . and the revolutionists triumphed: the workers were completely alienated from the czar and his government.[12]

Chaos followed as angry workers rioted in the streets of St. Petersburg and other cities. In Russian history the events of January 9, 1905, are known as Bloody Sunday.

Creation of the Duma

The shots fired at the crowd that day launched a long period of dissent in Russia that ultimately led to the abdication of the czar, establishment of a Communist regime, and the birth of the Soviet Union. Bloody Sunday also launched the 1905 Russian Revolution—a brief and largely unorganized uprising against the czar's government that was quickly put down.

Exiled from Russia, but nevertheless closely following the uprisings in St. Petersburg, was Vladimir Lenin. As the czar crushed the revolution, Lenin knew that it was only the beginning of what would be a long conflict and that, eventually, the czar's reign would come to an end. Soon after the events of Bloody Sunday, Lenin said:

> "The troops fired without rhyme or reason. There were hundreds of casualties . . . and the revolutionists triumphed: the workers were completely alienated from the czar and his government."[12]
>
> —Count Sergei Witte, witness to the Bloody Sunday shootings.

Before the uprising the [people] had been happy enough with the government. . . . [Then] the troops crushed unarmed workers, women and children. They shot people as they lay on the ground. With unutterable cynicism, they pronounced that they "had taught them a good lesson." The slaughter of 9 January changed everything. Even those Petersburg workers who had believed in the czar started to call for the immediate overthrow of the regime.[13]

Although the 1905 revolution failed, Nicholas recognized the dissent in his realm and pledged to make reforms. That October he issued the October Manifesto, granting Russian citizens a measure of civil rights and also creating a legislative branch of government—the Duma—composed of members elected by citizens. The following year a wide range of laws was codified into Russia's first constitution, in which the czar agreed to share power with the Duma.

The Tightfisted

But the czar was not as willing to cede power to the elected representatives of the Duma as the Russian people may have expected. Under the new constitution, the czar maintained many autocratic powers, including the right to overrule the Duma and enact laws of his own creation. Essentially, Russia's first constitution gave the czar the power to ignore the constitution. The Duma held its first session on April 27, 1906. Composed of reformers who believed their mission was to make the Russian government more responsible to the people, Duma members debated a number of measures to reform the government and military and provide land to the peasantry, but after ten weeks of debate the czar suddenly dissolved the Duma.

Nicholas wanted nothing to do with the widespread reforms proposed by the Duma, so he aimed to make the Duma more responsive to his desires. He ordered new elections for seats in the Duma but issued rules restricting voting rights to property owners. In the election of 1907, just 2 percent of Russia's 130 million people cast ballots for candidates to the Duma. Not surprisingly, the new Duma was composed of members whose first allegiance was to the czar—not to the citizens of Russia.

Some minor reforms were enacted by the new government. Pyotr Stolypin, the czar's chief minister, oversaw a modest land reform measure that provided poor farmers with some new land: Between

The Mad Monk

One of the most bizarre figures to surface during the final years of the reign of Nicholas II was Grigory Rasputin, a self-proclaimed holy man whose personality mesmerized Nicholas's wife, Alexandra. Born in the remote Siberian village of Pokrovskoye in 1872, Rasputin talked his way into joining the Imperial Court, claiming to be a monk. In fact, he was not ordained by any church. But Rasputin maintained a mystic influence over the empress because of his power to heal one of the Romanov children, Alexis Nikolayevich, the heir to the throne. Alexis was an ill child, believed to be a hemophiliac. Rasputin seemed to have the power to ease the boy's suffering.

But Rasputin also had an insatiable thirst for vodka and shunned the bath. His many affairs with the women of the Russian aristocracy—including, according to rumor, Empress Alexandra—infuriated members of the Imperial Court. To both the aristocracy and peasants of Russia, Rasputin—known as the Mad Monk—represented all that was wrong with the rule of the czar. "His carrying on with various society women, and his alleged carrying-on with the Empress herself, became a symbol for the political corruption of Russia," says London University history professor Orlando Figes. "For many people on the fringes of the court, Rasputin's corruption was taken as a cause of all of Russia's problems itself."

Rasputin was murdered on December 30, 1916. He was assassinated by a group of aristocrats who feared his conduct would stir rebellion against the czar.

Quoted in PBS, "Rasputin: The Cause of Russia's Problems," *The Great War and the Shaping of the 20th Century*, 2004. www.pbs.org.

1907 and 1915 land holdings of the peasantry grew from 4.3 billion acres to 4.6 billion acres (1.7 billion ha to 1.9 billion ha)—still only about half the agricultural land in Russia. The remaining land was owned by relatively few wealthy landowners—believed to number no more than 1 percent of the population. These landowners were known as kulaks—a slang term that translates roughly in English to "tightfisted."

Assassination in Sarajevo

Lenin was not alone in watching the unrest in Russia. In Germany, Kaiser Wilhelm II had long wanted to expand his country's influence over the European continent, particularly the Balkan states—small nation-states in Central Europe along the west coast of the Adriatic Sea. At the time, the Balkans were under the dominion of Austria-Hungary, a vast, unwieldy, and archaic empire ruled by Wilhelm's close ally, Austrian emperor Franz Josef. In 1914 a nationalist cell in the Balkan state of Serbia orchestrated the assassination of the emperor's son and heir, Archduke Franz Ferdinand, while the crown prince visited the Serbian city of Sarajevo.

Wilhelm urged Franz Josef to declare war on Serbia. But Serbia was populated by Slavs. Franz Josef knew attacking Serbia would mean risking war with Russia, which saw itself as protector of all Slavs. Wilhelm pledged Germany's aid to Austria-Hungary if Russia came to Serbia's defense. In August 1914 Austria-Hungary laid siege to Serbia, touching off World War I.

As Franz Josef expected, Russia mobilized to aid Serbia, and as Wilhelm promised, German troops engaged the Russians. But the Russians were as ill prepared for the Germans in 1914 as they had been for the Japanese in 1904. The Russian army was ill trained, poorly led, and lacked the arms to put up a good fight. As Russian losses mounted on the battlefield, the support of the Russian citizens for the cause quickly eroded. In March 1917 widespread labor strikes spread through St. Petersburg and other cities. Riots broke out in the streets. Throughout the cities, the czar kept storehouses filled with emergency supplies of grain and other foods; leaders of the Duma begged Nicholas to throw open the doors of the storehouses to feed the hungry people. Nicholas refused. Back on the streets, police officers sent to quell the riots threw down their guns and joined the rioters. On March 11, in a brazen act of defiance, the Duma proclaimed Nicholas no longer head of the Russian government and formed the Provisional Government. On March 15, realizing he had no alternative, Nicholas abdicated the throne of Russia.

Spreading Communism

In the streets the chaos was quelled as the Provisional Government opened the grain storehouses to feed the poor and hungry. In July the Duma selected one of its members, Alexander Kerensky, as prime minister. Kerensky oversaw a brief period of democracy in Russia, but in October a new revolution was sparked by the return of Lenin to Russia.

Lenin's rise to power marked the beginning of a Communist regime that held authority for the next seven decades. Following the ouster of the Kerensky government, Lenin and other Communist leaders abolished the Duma and established the Congress of Soviets as the government of Russia. More than one thousand representatives from soviets throughout Russia attended the first session of the

Lenin speaks at the first session of the Congress of Soviets in October 1917. The meeting, and Lenin's return to Russia, marked the establishment of the Bolshevik-dominated Soviet government.

> "Soldiers, workers in factory and office, the fate of the revolution and the fate of the democratic peace is in your hands! Long live the revolution!"[14]
>
> —Bolshevik leader Vladimir Lenin.

Congress. (The term *soviet* stems from the Russian word *suvetu*—meaning revolutionary or governing council.) These soviets were councils representing regions of Russia as well as factory workers, farmers, soldiers, craftspeople, and others. During the Congress, Lenin declared, "Soldiers, workers in factory and office, the fate of the revolution and the fate of the democratic peace is in your hands! Long live the revolution!"[14] And so began the long campaign by Communist leaders to provide the fruits of a classless society to the Russian people and to spread their vision of communism to lands and peoples well beyond Russian borders.

How Did Soviet Economic Policies Lead to Collapse?

Discussion Questions

1. Under what conditions might Joseph Stalin's collectivization of farms and nationalization of industry have succeeded?
2. Do you think productive farms and factories can exist in a classless society? If so, how so? If not, why not?
3. Even under the economic principles of communism, could the Soviet Union have found a way to prosper if it had maintained friendlier relations with the West?

The fall of the Soviet Union is regarded as an implosion—a rare occurrence in the annals of history. Over the centuries most countries that ceased to exist owed their failures to military defeat. Their armies were unable to defend their homelands, and as a result, these nations were conquered and absorbed by their enemies.

But that was not the case with the USSR. At the time of the 1991 collapse, the Soviet Union maintained one of the largest armies in the world. Moreover, Soviet leaders had access to an arsenal of nuclear weapons. No military had dared attack the Soviet Union since Hitler's failed invasion of 1941.

A major reason for the Soviet Union's collapse, experts agree, was the failure of the Communist economy. Unable to compete economically with the industrialized West, the USSR slowly ran out of food and other basic consumer goods. Raw materials to manufacture goods were in short supply, forcing Soviet citizens to lead modest lives with little hope of accumulating wealth or bettering their standards of living. And this circumstance occurred even though many of the countries that made up the Soviet Union, particularly Russia, sit atop some of the world's richest deposits of oil. But the Soviet Union's aggressive foreign policy, dedicated to spreading communism throughout the world, alienated countries from Western markets. Therefore, the Soviets found few Western customers for their oil.

Five-Year Plan

The Soviet Union's economic woes can be traced as far back as the 1920s. To make the USSR into a classless society, Lenin looked first at the rural regions. He appointed Committees of Poor Peasants charged with driving wealthy landowners, or kulaks, off their estates and farms. The peasants often employed violence to rid their villages of the kulaks, who left their land behind—and also left it fallow. These conflicts were fought in thousands of villages across the Soviet Union, and they resulted in a severe grain shortage because the former kulak farms stopped being productive.

Lenin responded by ordering the government to buy all available grain from the small farms still producing crops. The government set the prices, which stifled competition, providing little income for working farmers. By 1929 famine spread across the Soviet Union. Stalin was then in power, and he intended to solve the grain shortage by the "collectivization" of all agricultural land in the Soviet Union. In other words, thousands of small farms were joined together to form very large farms. Unlike the small, family-owned farms, these large farms could afford expensive farming machinery and the pay for laborers needed to till the crops.

The collectivization of farms was the centerpiece of Stalin's Five-Year Plan—his overall program, announced in 1928, to rescue the Soviet economy. "Agriculture is developing slowly, comrades," Stalin said as he announced the collectivization program. "This is because we have about 25 million individually owned farms. They are the most primitive and undeveloped form of economy. We must do our utmost to develop large farms and to convert them into grain factories for the country organised on a modern scientific basis."[15]

Vandalism and Insurrection

Only the most ardent Communists supported the Five-Year Plan. In the countryside many of the individual farmers, even those of the

Hopelessness shows in the faces of young, gaunt-faced famine victims in the Soviet Union in the 1920s. Millions died from famine resulting from measures first undertaken by Lenin and made markedly worse by Stalin's collectivization of farms.

most modest means, worked hard to accumulate their land and live-stock. Many farmers whose land was collectivized fled their properties, taking their belongings and farm animals with them. Farmers in Kazakhstan were particularly hostile to collectivization. By 1938 it is estimated the population of Kazakhstan dropped from 1.2 million households to fewer than 600,000. The Kazakh farmers went else-where rather than lose their belongings to collectivization. In 1929 authorities estimated there were 22 million sheep in Kazakhstan; by 1933 that number dropped to fewer than 2 million. Not until the 1960s did farming in Kazakhstan return to profitability. Elsewhere, farmers simply killed their livestock rather than permit the seizure of their animals by the collectives.

About 90 percent of Soviet farms had been collectivized by 1936, but the system never turned out to be the successful method of farm-ing Stalin had envisioned. Farmers who stayed toiled for low wages, earning far less than even the smallest farms before collectivization.

Moreover, work on a collective farm was mandatory—if the state ordered a Soviet citizen to work on a collective farm (regardless of his or her experience or other expertise), the citizen had no power to refuse. Over time the Soviet people came to view employment on collective farms as a form of serfdom.

Vandalism and insurrection were common on collective farms. To protest the low wages, workers killed livestock, smashed farm machinery, and sabotaged crops. With so much dissent boiling over on the collective farms, the system failed to alleviate the food shortages of the 1920s. In fact, during the 1930s the famine grew worse. British journalist Malcolm Muggeridge recalled touring collective farms during the 1930s: "This was in 1932, 1933, and I went down to the Ukraine and the Caucasus. . . . It was a scene of horror I had never seen before—villages with no one in them, peasants at a railway station being [shoved] off. People starving, people swollen. And it was awful, not least because it was manmade."[16]

> "It was a scene of horror I had never seen before—villages with no one in them, peasants at a railway station being [shoved] off. People starving, people swollen. And it was awful, not least because it was manmade."[16]
>
> —British journalist Malcolm Muggeridge, reporting on the famine of the 1930s.

State Control over Industry

The problems of small-time farming that Stalin said could be solved by collectivization did not go away simply because the farms were now bigger. Stalin insisted that larger farms would be able to afford expensive farm machinery, but such machinery was often in short supply. Soviet factories were poorly run and lacked raw materials needed to make the machines as well as replacement parts.

Indeed, another part of the Five-Year Plan was the nationalization of industries—meaning the government seized ownership of the nation's factories. As owner, the government then decided what products to produce, how much to produce, what prices to charge for merchandise, and how much to pay workers. This was communism in its purest form: state control over industry with the wealth

The Failure of Perestroika

Perestroika (restructuring) was Mikhail Gorbachev's chief economic initiative, designed to make Soviet industry more competitive with the West by giving factory managers more authority over production and prices. In reality perestroika was a modest reform. The Soviet government still held ultimate authority over industrial production and price fixing, meaning the factory managers had to work within a framework dictated by the government.

In fact, in a 1985 speech to political leaders in Soviet bloc countries, who were enduring their own economic woes, Gorbachev said, "Many of you see the solution to your problems in resorting to market mechanisms in place of direct planning. Some of you look at the market as a lifesaver for your economies. But, comrades, you should stop thinking about lifesavers and think about the ship: the ship is socialism."

Gorbachev did go on to make further reforms—in 1988 he signed the Law of Cooperatives, giving small entrepreneurs the right to own businesses. In the months following adoption of the law, new restaurants opened throughout Moscow and other Soviet cities. But Gorbachev's economic reforms never went far enough to rescue his country's failing economy. "Gorbachev made no secret of his aim—he wanted to reinvigorate the Soviet economy and Soviet society," says Martin Sixsmith, a former BBC correspondent who reported from the USSR. "It was just that he didn't know exactly how to do it."

Quoted in Martin Sixsmith, *Russia: A 1,000-Year Chronicle of the Wild East.* New York: Overlook, 2011, p. 450.

generated by factories distributed among workers, rather than into the pockets of a handful of wealthy capitalists. Or at least that was the theory.

Stalin wanted to see the Soviet economy recover as quickly as possible, so he ordered the new state-owned factories to increase production. To meet Stalin's high quotas, factories had to run twenty-four hours a day, seven days a week. This in turn brought an influx of workers to the cities in search of steady employment. They found jobs, but working conditions were poor and housing was in short supply. Says

Geoffrey Hosking, a professor of Russian history at the University of London:

> Finding a job was now not too difficult, since unemployment vanished early in the . . . Five Year Plan, but conditions at most workplaces were so grim that employees would quit pretty soon in order to find something less bad.... They would try to install their families in a room, provide food and clothing, and seek schooling for their children. Securing the simplest facilities required either bribery . . . or using "pull," the influence of a boss.[17]

A worker fulfills her daily tasks at a Soviet canning factory in 1940. Under Stalin, factory jobs were plentiful because factories ran all day, every day but working conditions were poor and housing hard to find.

Production Slows

In the factories production was hampered by the culture of the classless society installed by Lenin. Bosses were prohibited from giving orders, and committees of workers were supposed to resolve disputes and find ways to boost production. But infighting, political squabbling, and the general ineffectiveness of the system slowed everything down. Disruptions were common. Says Hosking, "At the Putilov [machinery] Works—and not only there—unpopular foremen would be trundled out in a wheelbarrow to be dumped in the street or even in a nearby river."[18]

By 1939 the Soviet Union was at war. Millions of men who worked on the collective farms or in the factories were conscripted into the military. Agricultural and industrial production suffered. Moreover, the food that was produced went first to the military, meaning many families had to endure the war years on the brink of starvation. When the war ended, the Soviet soldiers returned to their collective farms and factory jobs to find conditions little changed. They grumbled but went back to work.

> "At the Putilov [machinery] Works—and not only there—unpopular foremen would be trundled out in a wheelbarrow to be dumped in the street or even in a nearby river."[18]
>
> —Geoffrey Hosking, professor of Russian history at the University of London.

Culture of Idleness

Life on the collective farms and in the factories improved somewhat in 1956 when Nikita Khrushchev enacted a series of reforms. Wages remained low, but workers had opportunities to earn bonuses based on their production. Although workers believed they had incentives now to earn higher wages, Soviet farming and industry were still bogged down by many of the same problems that had been in existence for decades: Tractors could not be driven because parts were unavailable. Seeds and other supplies sat in warehouses because rail transportation was sporadic. Farm managers and factory foremen were often corrupt—falsifying production records in order to earn bonuses.

Also, the classless society of Lenin's era was still very much a way of life during Khrushchev's administration. Bosses still found them-

> "People . . . swap news, amuse themselves, do all kinds of things to preserve and improve their position, have contact with people on whom their well-being depends, go to innumerable meetings, get sent on leave to rest-homes, are assigned accommodations and sometimes supplementary food-products."[19]
>
> —Mathematician Aleksandr Zinoviev, describing the typical Soviet worker.

selves with limited authority on the factory floors—workers could turn down disagreeable jobs.

The pay for everyone was still low, but at least the government paid for health care and child care, and if one was homeless, the government provided housing. Since it was virtually impossible to be fired—the workers' committees protected everyone—few people were known to work hard. Studying the Soviet work environment in the 1950s, mathematician Aleksandr Zinoviev found a culture of idleness. Said Zinoviev, "People . . . swap news, amuse themselves, do all kinds of things to preserve and improve their position, have contact with people on whom their well-being depends, go to innumerable meetings, get sent on leave to rest-homes, are assigned accommodations and sometimes supplementary food-products."[19]

International Joke

By the 1960s the Soviet economy was something of an international joke. Western stand-up comics of the era got a lot of mileage out of poking fun at the Soviet economy. (A typical gag of the era: "In the Soviet Union, they pretend to pay us and we pretend to work."[20]) Moreover, Soviet foreign policy worked against the Soviet economy: The Cuban Missile Crisis, Soviet support for the North Vietnamese and Cuban Communists, and the proliferation of nuclear weapons within the USSR placed the country on hostile terms with the West. Therefore, trade between the Soviet Union and the United States and industrialized nations of Western Europe was unthinkable.

Khrushchev was ousted in 1964 by rivals in the Communist Party hierarchy dissatisfied with the country's economic morass and foreign policy disasters, most notably the Cuban Missile Crisis. Leonid Brezhnev, a hard-line and autocratic Communist, emerged as head of state. Believing that he could make the Soviet economy competitive with the West, Brezhnev funneled his country's resources into the production of steel, coal, and similar products needed to sustain heavy industry. He did not realize, though, that manufacturing was undergoing a metamorphosis in the West. During the 1960s technology took a great leap forward in the West as computers and new modes of communication were developed and refined. Evidence of the Soviet

Shopping in the Soviet Union

By the 1980s whenever a store in a Soviet city received new inventories of food, clothes, or other goods, word spread quickly. Shoppers dropped whatever they were doing to queue up for the goods. A system evolved in which shoppers had to stand in line three times for each purchase: the first time to view the product and learn the cost; the second to pay and get a receipt; the third to finally be handed the item. Waiting in line could take hours. It was common for shoppers to make it to the fronts of their lines and discover the products had been sold out.

In slow-moving lines, clever shoppers found others to hold their places, then queued up in faster-moving lines. Placeholders were obliged to defend the original shoppers' right to return against complaints from irritated shoppers in the rear. Says historian Katherine Bliss Eaton:

> Shopping was an unrelenting concern of most people's daily lives. Because there were constant shortages of everything except bread and vodka, people did not so much shop as forage for food and other common household purchases. As a Soviet woman pointed out . . . long lines were the norm for just about anything, including "a decent purse, a nice writing table, a good woman's bra—not a floppy, ugly Soviet one with no support and no adjustments, made for big-bosomed country girls, but a Czech bra or a Polish one, white and pretty instead of blue and baggy."

Katherine Bliss Eaton, *Daily Life in the Soviet Union.* Westport, CT: Greenwood, 2004, p. 116.

Union's lack of technological prowess could be found in the so-called race for the moon. In the early 1960s the United States and the Soviet Union both initiated ambitious programs to land astronauts on the moon. The United States won the race in 1969 when the *Apollo 11* spacecraft touched down on the moon, carrying two astronauts. As historians looked back at the moon race, they concluded that the Soviets never came close to developing the technology that would enable them to send a manned spacecraft to the moon.

Soon the Soviet Union found itself woefully behind in developing new and fast computers and methods of communication. By the 1980s, as the first mobile phones went into operation in cities in America and Western Europe, people in the Soviet Union were still using telephones with rotary dials. Moreover, since the state controlled all the wealth in the country, there were no entrepreneurial individuals who could put their ideas and managerial skills to use developing new technologies. In America entrepreneurs such as Steve Jobs at Apple and Bill Gates at Microsoft helped revolutionize Western technology. No such individuals existed in the Communist world.

Glasnost and Perestroika

Since the Soviets lacked trade partners and international markets for Soviet-made goods, little income was funneled into the country. As a result, food and consumer goods were hard to come by in the Communist countries. Familiar scenes on the streets of Moscow and other cities found long lines of consumers queuing up at stores. The lines often snaked for blocks.

Brezhnev died in 1982. He was succeeded by Yuri Andropov, former head of the KGB. Given Andropov's background as the nation's top spymaster, Western observers believed little would change in the Soviet Union: that the Communist regime would tolerate no reforms to make the country's economy more competitive with the West. In fact, though, Andropov was well aware of the dismal condition of his country's economy and pledged to make reforms. He cracked down on slackers by sending police into cinemas and taverns to find truant workers and force them to return to their jobs. He ordered corrupt bosses arrested and put on trial for falsifying production records.

An elderly Russian woman happily clutches the two loaves of bread she has just purchased. Others still await their turn in the long lines that became common in the Soviet Union in the 1980s and into 1991.

He also started the Soviet Union on a path toward a market-based economy, naming free-market proponents to top posts in the Soviet government bureaucracy.

But Andropov died in 1984, just fifteen months after taking power and initiating his reforms. A year later Mikhail Gorbachev emerged as the new general secretary of the Communist Party and president of the USSR. Gorbachev was convinced the Soviet Union could no longer sustain its Lenin-era economic policies. Said Gorbachev, "I, like many others, knew that the USSR needed radical change. If I had not understood this, I would never have accepted the position of General Secretary."[21]

Gorbachev initiated the programs of glasnost (openness) and perestroika (restructuring). Glasnost was an attempt to ease state control over the rights of Soviet citizens, giving them freedom of speech and other rights enjoyed by people in open societies. Perestroika was an attempt to restructure the Soviet economy by encouraging private entrepreneurship.

Failure of Communism

Soon Gorbachev found himself putting out fires across the Soviet bloc. Workers in Poland, led by shipyard worker Lech Walesa and the Solidarity movement, demanded human rights and economic freedoms denied them by the USSR. The popular uprising toppled the Soviet-backed Polish government in 1990. Similar uprisings unseated USSR-backed regimes in Romania, Czechoslovakia, Ukraine, and Lithuania. In 1990 Boris Yeltsin was elected president of the Russian Soviet Socialist Republic—the largest single state in the USSR—and banned the Communist Party in his country. In 1991 hard-line Communists attempted to stage a coup d'état against Gorbachev, but Yeltsin stepped in and won Gorbachev's release.

> "I, like many others, knew that the USSR needed radical change. If I had not understood this, I would never have accepted the position of General Secretary."[21]
>
> —Mikhail Gorbachev, the last general secretary of the Communist Party of the USSR and the last president of the USSR.

Gorbachev's remaining tenure as head of the Soviet Union was brief. On Christmas Day 1991, he resigned as general secretary. A short time later Yeltsin and the presidents of the former Soviet republics announced they had dissolved the Soviet Union and their countries were now independent states. These new states faced tremendous economic pressures. Their economies had deteriorated so much that in April 1992 the US Congress approved $24 billion in loans to the former Soviet Socialist Republics to help bail them out of their deep economic crises. During the depths of the Cold War, loans from the American people to the Soviet Union would have been unthinkable. Communism was now dead in the former Soviet Union—undone by a government's longtime commitment to an economic model that was as much a failure in the eras of Lenin and Stalin as it was in the time of Brezhnev, Andropov, and Gorbachev.

What Role Did the Cold War Weapons Buildup Play in the Soviet Collapse?

Discussion Questions

1. Why did Soviet leaders believe that the United States planned to attack the USSR, and were their fears justified?
2. Why did President Ronald Reagan continue investing in sophisticated and expensive weapons even after Mikhail Gorbachev's rise to power?
3. Do you think the collapse of the Soviet Union could have been avoided if Soviet leaders had resisted being drawn into the Cold War arms buildup? Explain your answer.

The year 1945 marked the end of World War II in both Europe and Asia. In the war against Japan, atomic bombs dropped by the United States on Hiroshima and Nagasaki decimated both cities and ended the war in Asia. Beyond ending the war, the bombings in Japan established the US military as the dominant fighting force on earth. No other country possessed the capability to wipe out an entire city with a single bomb.

That changed just four years later when the USSR conducted its first successful test of an atomic weapon. And so began the start of the Cold War and the emergence of the world's two nuclear-armed superpowers. Over the next four decades, both sides developed nuclear warheads with the capability to wipe out huge populations with a single blast. And the capacities to deliver these weapons—with intercontinental ballistic missiles (ICBMs), nuclear submarines, and long-range bombers—were developed as well. By the 1960s the USSR and the

United States held the capability to destroy not only each other, but all human civilization.

Mutually Assured Destruction

Although it was a tense era, to be sure, nuclear warfare never occurred, and the reason it never occurred could be attributed to a policy that emerged in the 1960s. It was known as mutually assured destruction—or MAD. This policy was first publicly explained in a 1967 speech by Defense Secretary Robert McNamara. Soviet authorities, he explained, needed to know that the United States would (and could) respond with maximum force in the event of a Soviet attack. To assure the capability to mount this response, the United States needed a stockpile of nuclear weapons. Said Mc-Namara:

> "The conclusion, then, is clear: if the United States is to deter a nuclear attack on itself or on our allies, it must possess an actual and a credible assured-destruction capability."[22]
>
> —US defense secretary Robert McNamara.

It is important to understand that assured destruction is the very essence of the whole deterrence concept. We must possess an actual assured-destruction capability, and that capability also must be credible. The point is that a potential aggressor must believe that our assured-destruction capability is in fact actual, and that our will to use it in retaliation to an attack is in fact unwavering. The conclusion, then, is clear: if the United States is to deter a nuclear attack on itself or on our allies, it must possess an actual and a credible assured-destruction capability.[22]

Essentially, under the policy of MAD, it was believed neither side would launch a nuclear attack because of the fear of retaliation by the other side. Such an attack and counterattack would reduce the two enemies—the United States and Soviet Union—to ashes. Throughout the 1960s and 1970s, political leaders in both nations lived under the policy, nervously content in the knowledge that the other side would never launch an attack. By the 1980s, though, the Soviets found good reason to believe that American leaders no longer feared nuclear combat with the USSR. And they also were convinced that if such a war was ever waged, they would lose.

Evil Empire

The roots of these Soviet fears could be found in the American election of 1980, which ushered in a new era in national politics. Ronald Reagan, a former Hollywood movie star and governor of California, was elected in a landslide. Reagan reflected a new conservative mindset in American thought—particularly when it came to dealing with America's enemies. The prior president, Jimmy Carter, preached a conciliatory tone in dealing with adversaries, insisting that diplomacy and negotiation should be the cornerstone of American foreign policy.

Reagan harbored much different ideas. He had no taste for negotiating with the Soviets, long regarded as America's enemies. Indeed, since the end of World War II the Soviets had dominated much of Eastern

Ronald Reagan, with his wife, Nancy, beside him, is sworn into the office of president in January 1981. As president, Reagan persuaded Congress to spend billions of dollars on weapons programs including the Strategic Defense Initiative, popularly known as Star Wars.

Europe while helping undermine American foreign policy in Latin America, Southeast Asia, Africa, and the Middle East. In those places, the Soviets aided Communist regimes or supplied weapons and other aid to governments hostile to the interests of the United States and its allies.

Moreover, by the 1980s the Soviets were regarded by most American as the lone nuclear power on earth capable, and willing, to launch ICBMs at American cities. By then seven countries were known to possess nuclear weapons. In addition to the United States and Soviet Union, the others were Great Britain, France, China, India, and Pakistan.

> "I urge you to beware the . . . temptation of blithely declaring yourselves above it all and label both sides equally at fault, to ignore the facts of history and the aggressive impulses of an evil empire."[23]
>
> —US president Ronald Reagan.

On March 8, 1983, Reagan addressed his position on the Soviet Union during a speech to a convention of evangelical Christian leaders in Orlando, Florida. At the time, a nuclear freeze movement had found traction in American society, led by activists who called on the US and Soviet governments to dismantle their nuclear weapons. Reagan spoke to the evangelical leaders, hoping to dissuade them from supporting the nuclear freeze movement. During the speech, he used strong and incendiary language against the Soviet Union, leaving no doubt that he regarded the Soviets as a threat to world peace:

> I urge you to speak out against those who would place the United States in a position of military and moral inferiority. . . . I urge you to beware the . . . temptation of blithely declaring yourselves above it all and label both sides equally at fault, to ignore the facts of history and the aggressive impulses of an evil empire, to simply call the arms race a giant misunderstanding and thereby removing yourself from the struggle between right and wrong and good and evil.[23]

Star Wars

Two weeks after Reagan delivered the speech labeling the Soviet Union an "evil empire," he announced an expensive, technologically advanced—and to his critics, far-fetched—program to protect Americans from nuclear attack. Known as the Strategic Defense Initiative (SDI), the plan included the launch of satellites into earth's orbit, each with the capability to destroy missiles in flight by blasting them with laser beams. The estimated cost of the program: at least $100 billion. Massachusetts senator Edward M. Kennedy, a political opponent of Reagan's, immediately gave SDI the nickname "Star Wars"—a reference to the popular series of science-fiction movies that featured enemies blasting

The Death of Star Wars

Fear of the Strategic Defense Initiative—dubbed Star Wars—forced the Soviet Union to spend its limited resources on new, expensive, and ultimately ineffective weaponry. SDI was envisioned as a system in which satellites armed with laser cannons could protect America and its allies from a Soviet missile attack. In fact, SDI was plagued by many technological challenges and therefore was never a threat to the security of the Soviet Union. After years of research and tens of billions of dollars in spending, American scientists and political leaders concluded the system was not viable given the tools available at the time—or even with the technology available today.

Research on SDI commenced in 1983 after Congress appropriated $30 billion to the project. The program was scaled down in the early 1990s following the collapse of the Soviet Union and was finally scrapped in 2009. Over the course of its twenty-six year history, though, SDI is estimated to have cost American taxpayers some $100 billion.

Although the project was a technological failure, proponents insist it accomplished its main goal: to help bring down the Soviet Union. Norman R. Augustine, former chair of the Lockheed Martin Corporation, an aeronautics company that won many contracts to develop weapons during the Reagan administration, admitted in 2004 that the Soviets had more faith in the success of SDI than the American engineers charged with developing the system. He said, "They were much more convinced we could make [SDI] work than many of us were, frankly."

Quoted in Greg Schneider and Renae Merle, "Reagan's Defense Buildup Bridges Military Eras," *Washington Post*, June 9, 2004. www.washingtonpost.com.

laser cannons in deep space combat. Kennedy's use of the term was derisive, meant to call attention to the fantastical nature of the program. But Kennedy's nickname for SDI was adopted by TV commentators and newspaper columnists, making the term *Star Wars*—when used to describe American defense policy—a part of everyday language.

Congress approved $30 billion in spending to launch the SDI program, but Reagan convinced American lawmakers to pour money into other weapons programs as well. Carter's administration had killed plans for the B-1 bomber, but Reagan revived development of the plane—an aircraft capable of delivering atomic bombs at supersonic speeds. Reagan also initiated development of the B-2 bomber, which featured stealth technology, meaning its approach to an enemy target would not show up on radar or other tracking systems. The MX missile was developed during Reagan's administration as well. After launch the MX deploys as many as ten separate warheads en route, meaning up to ten targets in the Soviet Union could be knocked out by a single missile.

President Reagan initiated development of the B-2 bomber (pictured). The aircraft features stealth technology that allows it to approach an enemy target without showing up on radar or other tracking systems.

Defense Spending Soars

These weapons were capable of delivering a degree of destruction never before witnessed in the history of the world. They were also very expensive. When Reagan took office in 1981 the defense budget—the amount of money Congress allocates to the military—stood at $444 billion. Reagan convinced Congress to hike the budget, and by 1984 the US defense budget stood at $580 billion. Defense spending slowed after its 1984 peak but never dipped below $500 billion while Reagan held office through early 1989.

During the Reagan years, membership in the four branches of service did not significantly increase—the ranks of the US Army, Navy, Air Force, and Marines remained at about 2 million during each of Reagan's eight years in office. Therefore, the increased spending was not concentrated on recruiting new members in the military but rather on new and technologically superior weapons systems such as SDI, the B-2 bomber, and MX missile.

Reagan poured so much money into new weaponry that he was forced to cut spending on social programs—such as school lunch programs for needy students and rental assistance to help keep homeless people off the streets. Soon after taking office in 1981, Reagan made it clear to members of his cabinet that defense spending and protecting Americans from a Soviet attack were the top priorities of his administration. "Look, I am the President of the United States; the commander in chief; my primary responsibility is the security of the United States," he told cabinet members. "If we don't have our security, we'll have no need for social programs."[24]

Autumn Forge

Reagan's defense policies were watched closely by Soviet leaders. Indeed, Reagan chose to announce development of SDI and pursue the other sophisticated weapons during a period of upheaval in the Soviet hierarchy. Brezhnev died five months before Reagan announced plans for SDI. Brezhnev's successor, Andropov, served just a brief term as the Soviet head of state. By the time Gorbachev ascended to power, SDI was well under development, and the US Congress was devoting more money to the military than it had ever committed in history.

This huge commitment to military spending by Congress, coupled with Reagan's strong rhetoric, raised fear among Soviet leaders. Many leaders in the Politburo firmly believed that Reagan was preparing his country for war against the Soviet Union—and that defeat was certain in the face of America's superior weapons. In 1982—soon after taking control of the Soviet government—Andropov ordered his country's intelligence agencies to begin gathering proof of what he believed was Reagan's ultimate plan: to launch a nuclear attack against the Soviet Union. The Soviet intelligence chiefs thought it unlikely that Reagan intended to launch such an attack. Nevertheless, they provided Andropov with whatever leads they could gather.

That information convinced an already-fearful Andropov and other Soviet leaders who shared his views that the Americans meant to attack the USSR. In 1983 the US military and its allies in Western Europe staged a series of ground maneuvers known as Autumn Forge. Some forty thousand members of the US and Western European militaries participated in Autumn Forge, which was described as a routine training mission for the troops. But Andropov and other Soviet leaders refused to believe Autumn Forge was anything less than a trial run—a preparation for the invasion of the Soviet Union. Indeed, communications by military officers that were recorded during Autumn Forge reflected orders to launch nuclear strikes. It is very likely that Soviet intelligence officers intercepted those communications, making them available to the Soviet hierarchy. Says Douglas Birch, the former Moscow bureau chief for the Associated Press, "The script for the maneuvers dovetailed snugly and perilously with the Soviets' fears that they were under threat, coupled with nagging doubts about their ability to protect themselves from US military might."[25]

> "The script for the [Autumn Forge] maneuvers dovetailed snugly and perilously with the Soviets' fears that they were under threat, coupled with nagging doubts about their ability to protect themselves from US military might."[25]
>
> —Douglas Birch, former Moscow bureau chief for the Associated Press.

Lack of Engineering Skills

Over the years, the hawks in the Politburo had pressed Brezhnev, Andropov, and Gorbachev to keep pace with the United States in weapons

The Bombing Begins in Five Minutes

On August 11, 1984, President Ronald Reagan did his part to stoke the fears of the Soviets when he announced—in jest—that he intended to order the bombing of Soviet cities. Reagan uttered these words as he prepared to deliver his weekly radio address, broadcast on National Public Radio.

Before the broadcast, the radio engineer asked Reagan to say a few words—to provide a sound check so the engineer could adjust the volume to better project the voice of the speaker. Reagan complied and—believing his words were not being recorded—uttered a farcical statement that nevertheless sent shock waves throughout the Soviet hierarchy: "My fellow Americans, I'm pleased to tell you today that I've signed legislation that will outlaw Russia forever. We begin bombing in five minutes."

The Soviets did not get the joke. In fact, a Japanese newspaper reported that after the comment leaked out, Soviet troops were placed on high alert. Eventually, the troops were recalled, but tempers did not cool. Said a TV commentator for a Moscow news show, "Reagan blurts out what he is thinking, that is, to outlaw Russia and to start bombing in five minutes. This is a joke. But this is also a secret dream which was allowed to escape. It is simple-mindedness, mildly speaking, which characterizes the view of the president on world problems." The White House never apologized for Reagan's comments—a fact that further infuriated the Soviets.

Quoted in Ed Adamczyk, "Flashback: Reagan Jokes About Bombing Soviet Union, 30 Years Ago," UPI, August 11, 2004. www.upi.com.

development. Brezhnev did not need much convincing. Since ascending to power he spent liberally on the military, aiming to make the Soviet armed forces the best-equipped in the world. Even as the Soviet Union's economy began its downward spiral, Brezhnev refused to rein in military spending. "As early as the 1970s some officials warned Leonid Brezhnev that the economy would stagnate if the military continued to consume such a disproportionate share of resources," write political scientists Richard Ned Lebow and Janice Gross Stein. "[Brezhnev] ignored their warnings. . . . Brezhnev was . . . extraordinarily loyal to the Soviet military and fiercely proud of its performance."[26] Andropov maintained a high level of spending on the military as well.

But as the Soviets spent heavily on new weapons, they had little to show for their efforts. Lacking the engineering and scientific skills of American military contractors, the most significant weapon produced by the Soviet Union during the 1970s and 1980s was the SS-20, a medium-range missile armed with a nuclear warhead that could be launched from the bed of a flatbed truck. The SS-20 gave the Soviets the ability to move missiles around their European borders—but with SDI under development by the Americans, the ability to deliver an SS-20 warhead to a target was no longer a certainty. Many Soviet leaders feared that they had lost the Cold War—that MAD was no longer a viable deterrent and that if attacked by the United States and its allies, the Soviet Union would lose. With SDI protecting the United States and its allies against counterattack, the Soviets concluded they were powerless to stop an American attack.

A Treaty Too Late

Gorbachev did not share the view that a US attack was imminent or that the Americans were even planning such an attack. Improving the lot of the Soviet people concerned him far more than whether his country could survive a nuclear war. Gorbachev realized that the real threat lay in the country's economic crisis; he believed the high level of defense spending was sapping the USSR's resources. The enormous amount of money the US government spent on defense during the Reagan years is a matter of public record, but in the secret world of the Soviet government, such numbers were hard to come by. Experts such as Wayne State University professor Moti Nissani acknowledge that it is impossible to know how much the Soviets spent trying to match the Reagan administration's commitment to the arms buildup.

He suggests, however, that some comparisons can be made. During the height of the Reagan era, military spending cost each American taxpayer $5,000 a year. Given that the standard of living for a Soviet citizen was well below that of the average American, Nissani says, the toll the USSR's military budget took on the average Soviet citizen must have been far more burdensome. "In the Soviet Union,

In December 1987, Mikhail Gorbachev, president of the Soviet Union, and Ronald Reagan, president of the United States, sign an agreement to eliminate medium-range missiles from the arsenals of both countries.

the burden [of military spending] has been far heavier," he says. "First, throughout most of the Cold War, the costs of the arms race had been laughingly under-reported by the Soviet government. Second, owing to the greater poverty and technological backwardness of the Soviet Union, Soviet citizens paid a higher price for the arms race than American citizens."[27]

Gorbachev knew the arms race had to end—that it was bankrupting the USSR. Soon after attaining power he called on Reagan to negotiate an arms reduction treaty. In 1987 the two leaders met in Washington and agreed to eliminate medium-range missiles from the arsenals of both countries. This included US Pershing missiles and Soviet SS-20 missiles. Gorbachev had further hoped to convince Reagan to scrap SDI, but the American president refused.

By now the Soviet Union's economy was stumbling badly. Gorbachev hoped to open trade with the West but knew many of the Western democracies would refuse to engage in trade with his country as long as they viewed the Soviet Union as a military threat. And so he was forced to agree to Reagan's terms. Says Gennady Gerasimov, who served as top spokesperson for the Soviet Foreign Ministry during the 1980s, "Reagan bolstered the US military might to ruin the Soviet economy, and he achieved his goal. . . . Reagan's SDI was a very successful blackmail. The Soviet Union tried to keep up pace with the US military buildup, but the Soviet economy couldn't endure such competition."[28]

> "Reagan's SDI was a very successful blackmail. The Soviet Union tried to keep up pace with the US military buildup, but the Soviet economy couldn't endure such competition."[28]
>
> —Gennady Gerasimov, spokesperson for the Soviet Foreign Ministry.

Gorbachev got his treaty, but by then it was too late. The American arms buildup had pushed Soviet leaders to respond in kind during a period when the Soviet Union could ill afford such expenditures. By the time the Soviet Union collapsed in 1991, no B-2 bomber had ever flown into Soviet airspace. No MX missile was ever fired at a Soviet city. And SDI turned out to be the fantastical project Kennedy said it was—no laser-shooting satellites have ever been launched into space. The program was eventually scrapped. But in a futile attempt to match the development of American weaponry, the Soviets spent their limited resources and, in the process, destroyed their economy and their country.

How Did the Collapse of the Soviet Union Lead to War and Ethnic Conflict?

Discussion Questions

1. In what ways did the Soviet Union's creation and demise contribute to ethnic conflict?
2. As the Soviet Union headed toward collapse, what steps could Soviet leaders have taken to ease tensions among the various ethnic groups that for decades coexisted on hostile terms?
3. Do you think the fall of the Soviet Union provides an opportunity for peace and prosperity for both Russia and Ukraine? If so, how so? If not, why not?

Joseph Stalin used his country's military to expand the borders of the USSR, invading and absorbing neighboring nations. By 1940 the Soviet Union had grown to encompass fifteen Soviet Socialist Republics. Among the new Soviet citizens were millions of people from numerous ethnic groups: Inuits from the northernmost regions of the USSR; Slavs from the Eastern European republics of Ukraine, Estonia, and Latvia; Uzbeks and the Kyrgyz, peoples of Turkish ethnicity; Tajiks, whose ancestry can be traced to ancient Persia; and Mongols, an ethnic group with roots in Asian countries. The USSR was also home to people of many faiths: Roman Catholics, Russian Orthodox Christians, Jews, Muslims, and Buddhists, among others.

When Stalin's troops invaded these lands, they often found them already embroiled in strife, their peoples engaged in conflicts dating back centuries. In many of these new Soviet republics, people of diverse ethnicities and religions had lived amongst one another on hostile terms. But once the Soviet Union absorbed a country into its domain, the Communist regime tolerated no dissent. Stalin did not want a nation of diverse ethnic groups—he wanted a nation of dedicated Communists. When long-standing and bitter rivalries among ethnic or religious groups flared up, the government in Moscow quickly dispatched troops to quell the discord. Says James B. Minahan, an author and expert on ethnic conflict, "Assimilation policies . . . stressed the homogenization of the population of the new Soviet Empire and the disappearance of all ethnic and national identification except that of the government's newly fabricated Soviet identity. . . .Traditional national cultures were vilified as anti-Communist."[29]

Ethnic Hostility in Kyrgyzstan

Just because the Communist government tolerated no infighting does not mean hard feelings were forgotten. For decades, ethnic strife remained a part of life in the Soviet Union, quietly festering below the surface. When the USSR collapsed, the tight reins kept on these warring factions disappeared—and warfare erupted. One of the first places to explode in violence was the Central Asian nation of Kyrgyzstan.

In 1990, a year before the breakup of the USSR, fighting broke out in what was then the Kyrgyz Soviet Socialist Republic between two ethnic groups: native Kyrgyz and ethnic Uzbeks. The dispute in Kyrgyzstan has its roots in the original takeover of the Central Asian nation by the Soviets in the 1920s and the transformation of a Kyrgyz region known as the Fergana Valley into collective farms. Russians and Uzbeks migrated to the Fergana Valley looking for work. Soon the native Kyrgyz citizens found themselves in the minority.

The Russians started leaving in the late 1980s when it grew evident the Soviet Union was on the verge of collapse, leaving the ethnic Uzbeks as the majority population in the Fergana Valley. In 1990 a movement led by Kyrgyz insurgents demanded the collective farms be broken up and the land awarded to the native citizens. Fighting broke out between the Kyrgyz and Uzbeks, but quick action by Soviet troops quelled the violence.

After the Soviet collapse, the Kyrgyz Soviet Socialist Republic declared its independence, taking the name Kyrgyzstan. By 2010 ethnic strife resurfaced, flaring into violence in the southern Kyrgyzstan city of Osh. By then no Soviet troops were available to take control of the troubled city. As a result, a full-scale civil war erupted, taking the lives of two thousand people while displacing more than three hundred thousand refugees from their homes in and near the city.

Violence in Osh

Following the breakup of the USSR, the Kyrgyz government eliminated the collective farms, returning them to private ownership. Native Kyrgyz flocked to the Fergana Valley, renewing their demands for farmland and calling on the government to deny land to the ethnic Uzbeks. By the late 1990s the population of the Fergana Valley and its largest city, Osh, had reached about 2.7 million people—with 70 percent of the citizens now Kyrgyz.

This conflict between the Kyrgyz and Uzbeks involved more than just a dispute over land. The Kyrgyz and Uzbeks are both of Central Asian ethnicity, but their cultures are vastly different. Dating back to

Soldiers in armored vehicles patrol the streets of Osh in Kyrgyzstan in 2010. Violence between native Kyrgyz and ethnic Uzbeks erupted in Osh as a result of disputes over land and in response to political persecution and government corruption.

Turmoil in Chechnya

Since the collapse of the USSR, Russia has had to respond to strife in the region known as Chechnya. When the USSR collapsed in 1991, dissidents called for the Russian government to grant independence to Chechnya, located in southern Russia. Chechens want independence because they regard themselves as culturally different from Russians. They are predominantly Muslims, not Russian Orthodox Christians, and they are not Russian speakers.

Street fighting erupted in 1994. The Russian government responded by sending troops into Chechnya. Troops returned in 1999 when violence resumed; since then the Russian army has maintained a heavy presence in Chechnya. Nevertheless, acts of terrorism are common, and violence has spilled over elsewhere in Russia. In 2002 forty Chechen terrorists seized the Dubrovka Theatre in Moscow, holding nine hundred people hostage. After a three-day standoff, Russian commandos stormed the theater—using fentanyl, an opiate-based gas, to sedate the terrorists. All 40 terrorists died by commando fire, but 130 of the hostages also died—most from the effects of the gas.

More than a dozen years later, unrest in Chechnya continues. In 2013 Russian leaders believed they struck a blow against the insurgents when commandos killed rebel leader Doku Umarov. But in October 2014 a suicide bomber in the Chechen capital of Grozny blew himself up, killing five police officers. The bomber ignited the explosive during a police search as he attempted to enter a concert hall. Police theorize the bomber aimed to kill hundreds attending the concert.

the era of explorer Marco Polo in the thirteenth century, the Uzbeks have regarded themselves as traders and merchants while believing the Kyrgyz to be a nomadic people who make their homes in large tents known as yurts. "We're hardworking people," an Uzbek from the city of Cheremushki told the London *Guardian* newspaper. "We never lived in yurts. For the past 2,000 years we've built stone houses. Since [Marco Polo's era] we've been involved in commerce and trade. We are successful. The Kyrgyz people are jealous and resent this."[30]

Kyrgyz president Kurmanbek Bakiyev, who took power in 2005, stripped many Uzbeks of their land and also permitted persecution of the Uzbeks. Bakiyev ruled Kyrgyzstan as a strongman, stifling dissent, closing opposition newspapers, tossing political opponents in jail, and rigging elections to ensure his reelection. By April 2010 the Kyrgyz people had had enough of his dictatorship and, following a series of violent protests, drove Bakiyev from power.

The real losers in this turmoil, however, were Kyrgyzstan's ethnic Uzbeks. A month after Bakiyev's ouster, violence exploded in Osh. Kyrgyz mobs targeted the Uzbeks, burning their homes and businesses, assaulting individuals, and driving the Uzbeks from the Fergana Valley. The Kyrgyz military responded and, after several weeks of violence, was able to bring order to Osh and other communities in the Fergana Valley.

Five years after the violence, the Kyrgyz military remains a presence in the Fergana Valley, but ethnic Uzbeks still insist they are intimated by the Kyrgyz. In 2013 a United Nations study accused the government of ignoring the abuse of the Uzbeks, reporting that Kyrgyz citizens arrested for intimidating Uzbeks are typically given light sentences or found innocent of the charges by biased Kyrgyz courts.

> "We're hardworking people. We never lived in yurts. For the past 2,000 years we've built stone houses. . . . We are successful. The Kyrgyz people are jealous and resent this."[30]
>
> —An ethnic Uzbek citizen of Kyrgyzstan.

Strife Between Christians and Muslims

The violence in Kyrgyzstan could be categorized as a civil war because the fighting has been confined to ethnic groups within that country. In another case the former Soviet Socialist Republics of Armenia and Azerbaijan waged war when a long-standing treaty brokered decades ago by Bolshevik leaders collapsed after the breakup of the USSR in 1991. Without the powerful presence of the Soviet military to keep the peace between Armenia and Azerbaijan, ethnic and religious conflicts between the two countries led to warfare followed by a stalemate. By late 2014 hostilities had still not been resolved.

As in the case of Kyrgyzstan, the war that erupted in 1991 between Armenia and Azerbaijan can be traced to the Soviet Union's invasion of the two countries in the 1920s. The Soviets hoped to use the two strategically located countries to launch attacks against Turkey under a plan to make Turkey into a Soviet Socialist Republic.

At the heart of their dispute is the region of Nagorno-Karabakh, an autonomous area within Azerbaijan populated by an Armenian majority. Nagorno-Karabakh was created by the Bolsheviks in 1920. When the Soviets invaded Azerbaijan, they found a civil war underway between the Christian Armenians and Muslim Azeris. To end the civil war, they created the autonomous region of Nagorno-Karabakh and convinced both sides to agree to a truce. The cease-fire was supposed to be temporary, giving the new Soviet government the opportunity to divide the land between the two sides. In the meantime the Armenians and Azeris found themselves living side by side in Nagorno-Karabakh as hostile neighbors.

Street Combat

Moscow was never able to bring Turkey into the Communist sphere. Turkey aligned with the West, giving permanence to what was supposed to be the temporary zone of Nagorno-Karabakh even though the ethnic and religious strife between the Armenians and Azeris continued. Over the years, whenever tensions flared the Soviet army was always quick to respond, tamping down violence and ethnic tension.

In 1988, as Soviet influence declined, friction between Armenians and Azeris in Nagorno-Karabakh exploded into street combat. That year the parliament in Nagorno-Karabakh voted to join Armenia. Fighting broke out in the streets; as many as thirty thousand Armenians and Azeris died in the conflict. Eventually, the ethnic Armenian majority gained control of Nagorno-Karabakh, pushing farther into Azerbaijan, creating a buffer zone around the region, and providing a geographic link between Nagorno-Karabakh and Armenia. In 1991, when the Soviet Union ceased to exist, the Nagorno-Karabakh parliament declared the region an independent state under the name of Karabakh.

Azerbaijan responded by attacking Karabakh. Armenia joined the fray, invading Azerbaijan. During the fighting, the Azeris of Karabakh fled their homes, finding refuge in Azerbaijan; the Armenians of Azerbaijan fled as well, taking refuge in Armenia or Karabakh. As many as 1 million people have been displaced during the conflict.

Surrounded by all of her earthly possessions, an elderly Armenian woman awaits help in Azerbaijan in May 1991. Thousands have died in a bloody ethnic and religious conflict involving Azerbaijan, Armenia, and a region called Nagorno-Karabakh.

Fighting continued into 1994, when Russia brokered a peace treaty, leaving the region under Armenian control. The treaty was intended to be temporary as the two sides sought a lasting peace. By late 2014, however, there had been no break in the stalemate. Both sides have stationed troops along their common border, and it is not uncommon for clashes to erupt. Since 1994 as many as sixty soldiers have been killed by shots fired across the border. In November 2014 tensions escalated when an Armenian army helicopter was shot down over the border by Azeri soldiers who claimed the aircraft fired at them. Three Armenian crew members were killed. Armenian officials insisted the attack on the aircraft was unprovoked. Said Artsrun Hovannisyan, a spokesperson for the Armenian Foreign Ministry, "This is an unprecedented escalation and the consequences for Azerbaijan will be grave."[31]

For their part, the Azeris are willing to stand firm against Armenia. Elham Mammadov, a nineteen-year-old member of the Azeri army assigned to the border, says he is willing to cross the border to wage war against the Armenians. He says, "I'm very proud to serve my

Dictatorship in Kazakhstan

For the people of the former Kazakh Soviet Socialist Republic, now known as Kazakhstan, life is not much different than what they knew under the Communist regime. The country is a totalitarian state led by a dictator, Nursultan Nazarbayev, who has held power since the Soviet collapse. As president, Nazarbayev has stood for election several times. He typically wins with at least 95 percent of the vote; human rights groups say the elections are rigged.

Nazarbayev tolerates no dissent. In 2012, after dissidents organized a labor strike at an oil field, Nazarbayev ordered the demonstration smashed. Thirty-seven dissidents were arrested. According to a report by the human rights group Amnesty International, the dissidents were tortured. Female arrestees were raped in custody. Finally, the dissidents were put on trial and sentenced to lengthy prison terms.

In another case Mukhtar Dzhakishev—an official in Kazakhstan's uranium industry—was arrested in 2009 as he prepared to attend a meeting with a Japanese delegation seeking to buy uranium mined in Kazakhstan. His daughter, Aigerim, believes her father had somehow run afoul of Nazarbayev. Dzhakishev was convicted on what his daughter describes as trumped-up embezzlement charges. His prison sentence expires in 2023. Says Aigerim, "My father was a successful, respected and powerful public figure in Kazakhstan. . . . If he can be taken away, convicted of fanciful charges and abused indefinitely in a penal colony, then the message is clear: anyone can be. And they often are."

Aigerim Dzhakisheva, "Kazakhstan Is an Abusive Dictatorship—the UK Should Not Court It," *Guardian* (London), May 21, 2014. www.theguardian.com.

homeland. And every day, every hour, I want the war to start, so that we can liberate our homeland from the Armenian aggressor."[32]

Gangster Capitalism

Unlike the conflicts involving the Kyrgyz and Uzbeks or the Armenians and Azeris, there is nothing ethnic nor religious about what has been, perhaps, the most serious threat to peace in Eastern Europe since the collapse of the Soviet Union. In 2014 troops from Russia invaded Ukraine. Russia has also backed an insurrection in Ukraine by providing arms to antigovernment dissidents. The cause of the conflict is largely economic: Russia fears that its longtime trading partner will instead begin doing business with the industrialized nations of the West, leading to a crippling of the Russian economy. As part of the old USSR, what had been the Ukrainian Soviet Socialist Republic would never have been free to strike independent trade deals with the West.

The cause of the conflict between Russia and Ukraine can be traced to the rise of what is known as "gangster capitalism" in Russia following the breakup of the Soviet Union. In the years following the collapse of the USSR, enormous wealth was concentrated into the hands of a small cadre of billionaires who exercise near total control over the Russian economy.

These billionaires gained their wealth by exploiting their relationships with Boris Yeltsin, who—despite his heroism in engineering the collapse of the Soviet Union—headed a new government in Russia that was highly susceptible to corruption. By the time Yeltsin stepped down as president of Russia in 1999, a handful of Russian billionaires had taken control of a large proportion of the country's wealth. They are well served by the Russian president, Vladimir Putin, who under the old Soviet regime served in the KGB and then, after the collapse of the Soviet Union, found a bureaucratic job in the city government of St. Petersburg. But the savvy Putin rose in power and in 2000 ascended to the presidency of Russia. Along the way he used his political power to accumulate massive wealth and is reported to be worth $70 billion.

> "I'm very proud to serve my homeland. And every day, every hour, I want the war to start, so that we can liberate our homeland from the Armenian aggressor."[32]
>
> —Nineteen-year-old Azeri soldier Elham Mammadov.

Meanwhile, the Russian middle class is just modestly better off than it was during the classless society of the Soviet years. The Ukrainians, on the other hand, are anxious to exploit their vast natural gas reserves and rich agricultural lands. In 2013 the Ukrainians made overtures to join the European Union (EU), the association of European countries that share a common currency and economy—a move that would open Ukraine to investment by the West.

Riots in Kiev

Putin saw the dangers to the Russian economy should Ukraine join the EU. In late 2013 Putin pressured Ukrainian president Viktor Yanukovych to cancel his country's plans to join the EU. Since the breakup of the Soviet Union, the Ukrainian and Russian economies have been closely tied, and the two countries are trading partners. Putin feared that if Ukraine joined the EU, the country would turn to the West to buy its consumer goods—invariably cheaper and of better quality than Russia provides. Also, Putin feared these goods would flow through Ukraine into Russia, opening a huge consumer market to the West and robbing Russia's industries—controlled by the Russian billionaire oligarchy—of revenue.

When Yanukovych canceled the EU offer, rioters took to the streets of Kiev, the Ukrainian capital. Clashes between protesters and police continued for months, until the protesters succeeded in driving Yanukovych from power. In the months following the ouster of

Ukrainians hold long lengths of cloth in the yellow and blue colors of the nation's flag while rallying against Russia's annexation of Crimea in March 2014.

Yanukovych (who fled to Russia), Russia has made it clear it intends to maintain control over Ukraine. In March 2014 Russia sent troops across the border to annex the Crimea, a peninsula in Ukraine, while pro-Russian insurgents armed with Russian weapons staged a civil war in eastern Ukraine.

A New Cold War

Although their country has been under siege since the Russian invasion, Ukrainians have refused to yield. In June 2014 Petro Poroshenko was elected president of Ukraine and vowed to join the EU. The Ukrainians have found widespread support around the globe. Many European countries and the United States have imposed trade embargoes on Russia. By late 2014 Putin was forced to admit that the trade sanctions had a devastating effect on his country's economy. Still, the Russian troops remained in Crimea, and the civil war in eastern Ukraine continued.

Moreover, Putin has threatened to use nuclear weapons to ensure Russia's interests in Ukraine are preserved. "I want to remind you that Russia is one of the most powerful nuclear nations," Putin told Russian journalists in August 2014. "This is a reality, not just words."[33]

> "I want to remind you that Russia is one of the most powerful nuclear nations. This is a reality, not just words."[33]
>
> —Russian president Vladimir Putin.

Putin's boastful rhetoric about deploying nuclear weapons conjures up memories of an era when the US and USSR relied on the policy known as MAD to keep each other's aggressions in check. While ethnic and religious tensions have been confined to the former Soviet Socialist Republics, economic disputes have gone beyond those borders and prompted new talk about waging nuclear war. More than two decades after the breakup of the USSR, the countries of the former Soviet Union continue to be dominated by ethnic, religious, and economic differences that date back decades. Without the strong arm of the central Soviet government to keep these hostilities in check, the future for these former Soviet states will likely be embroiled in hostility and bloodshed for many years to come.

Introduction: End of the Cold War

1. Ronald Reagan, *An American Life*. New York: Threshold, 1990, p. 258.
2. Quoted in Francis X. Clines, "Committee Formed: 'Health Reasons' Cited—No Word from Vacationing Leader," *New York Times*, August 19, 1991, p. A1.
3. Quoted in Tony Karon and James O. Jackson, "Boris Yeltsin: The Man Atop the Tank," *Time*, March 23, 2007. http://content.time.com.

Chapter One: A Brief History of the Soviet Union's Collapse

4. Karl Marx and Friedrich Engels, *The Communist Manifesto*. New York: Washington Square, 1970, p. 116.
5. Ronald Clark, *Lenin: The Man Behind the Mask*. (E-book, Kindle edition.) London: Bloomsbury, 2011.
6. Quoted in Walter Laqueur, *The Dream That Failed: Reflections on the Soviet Union*. New York, Oxford University Press, 1994, p. 6.
7. Quoted in David Welch, *Hitler: Profile of a Dictator*. New York, Routledge, 2001, p. 74.

Chapter Two: How Did Czarist Policies Contribute to the Rise of Communism?

8. Richard Charques, *The Twilight of Imperial Russia*. Oxford: Oxford University Press, 1965, p. 14.
9. Quoted in William Simpson and Martin Jones, *Europe, 1783–1914*. New York: Routledge, 2009, p. 222.
10. Quoted in Martin Sixsmith, *Russia: A 1,000-Year Chronicle of the Wild East*. New York: Overlook, 2012, p. 160.
11. Quoted in Geoffrey Hosking, *Russia and the Russians: A History*. Cambridge, MA: Harvard University Press, 2001, p. 366.
12. Quoted in Sixsmith, *Russia*, pp. 160–61.
13. Quoted in Sixsmith, *Russia*, p. 162.
14. Vladimir Lenin, "To Workers, Soldiers and Peasants," Marxists Internet Archive, October 25, 1917. www.marxists.org.

Chapter Three: How Did Soviet Economic Policies Lead to Collapse?

15. Quoted in History Learning Site, "Collectivisation of Agriculture in Russia," 2014. www.historylearningsite.co.uk.
16. Quoted in Sixsmith, *Russia*, p. 263.
17. Hosking, *Russia and the Russians*, pp. 457–58.
18. Hosking, *Russia and the Russians*, p. 396.
19. Quoted in Hosking, *Russia and the Russians*, p. 537.
20. Quoted in Alan Caruba, "Living in a Communist Economy," *Canada Free Press*, July 21, 2013. http://canadafreepress.com.
21. Quoted in Richard Ned Lebow and Janice Gross Stein, "Reagan and the Russians," *Atlantic*, February 1994. www.theatlantic.com.

Chapter Four: What Role Did the Cold War Weapons Buildup Play in the Soviet Collapse?

22. Quoted in Atomic Archive, "'Mutual Deterrence' Speech by Sec. of Defense Robert McNamara," 2013. www.atomicarchive.com.
23. Quoted in Paul Kengor, *The Crusader: Ronald Reagan and the Fall of Communism*. New York: HarperCollins, 2006, p. 173.
24. Quoted in Peter Schweizer, *Reagan's War: The Epic Story of His Forty-Year Struggle and Final Triumph over Communism*. New York: Anchor, 2003, pp. 139–40.
25. Douglas Birch, "The USSR and US Came Closer to Nuclear War than We Thought," *Atlantic*, May 28, 2013. www.theatlantic.com.
26. Lebow and Gross Stein, "Reagan and the Russians."
27. Moti Nissani, "Lives in the Balance: the Cold War and American Politics, 1945–1991," Wayne State University, 1992. www.is.wayne.edu.
28. Quoted in NBC News, "In Russia, Reagan Remembered for Helping Bring Down Soviet Union," June 5, 2004. www.nbcnews.com.

Chapter Five: How Did the Collapse of the Soviet Union Lead to War and Ethnic Conflict?

29. James B. Minahan, *The Former Soviet Union's Diverse Peoples: A Reference Sourcebook*. Santa Barbara, CA: ABC-CLIO, 2004, p. 156.

30. Quoted in Luke Harding, "Kyrgyzstan Killings Are Attempted Genocide, Say Ethnic Uzbeks," *Guardian* (London), June 16, 2010. www.theguardian.com.

31. Quoted in BBC, "Armenian Helicopter Downing: 'Grave Consequences' Warning," November 13, 2014. www.bbc.com.

32. Quoted in Damien McGuinness, "Azerbaijan Armenia: Karabakh's Smouldering Conflict," BBC News, December 15, 2012. www.bbc.com.

33. Quoted in Greg Botelho and Laura Smith-Spark, "Putin: You Better Not Come After a Nuclear-Armed Russia," CNN, August 30, 2014. www.cnn.com.

Books

Todd Chretien, ed., *State and Revolution by Vladimir Lenin*. Chicago: Haymarket, 2014.

Karl Marx and Frederick Engels, *The Communist Manifesto*. New York: International, 2014.

Serhii Plokhy, *The Last Empire: The Final Days of the Soviet Union*. New York: Basic Books, 2014.

Robert Service, *Spies and Commissars: The Early Years of the Russian Revolution*. New York: Public Affairs, 2012.

Martin Sixsmith, *Russia: A 1,000-Year Chronicle of the Wild East*. New York: Overlook, 2012.

Websites

Cold War Museum (www.coldwar.org). The website maintained by the museum in Vint Hill, Virginia, includes a timeline of events in the years between the end of World War II and the collapse of the Soviet Union. Online features also include videos and photos depicting life in the USSR and a trivia game challenging students to test their knowledge of communism and related topics.

House of Romanov (www.imperialhouse.ru/eng). Maintained by the surviving members of the Romanov family, the website chronicles the Romanov dynasty, which ruled Russia from 1613 until the abdication of Nicholas II in 1917. The site includes a history of the Romanov czars and an explanation of the laws granting imperial rule to the Romanovs.

Iron Curtain Trail (www.ironcurtaintrail.eu/en). Established by European political leaders, the website enables visitors to take a virtual tour of the Iron Curtain, the imaginary but well-policed border between the Soviet bloc countries and the free democracies of the West. Students can find photos from the Iron Curtain era and download maps as well as a history of the era.

Marxist Internet Archive (MIA) (www.marxists.org). Dedicated to chronicling the history of Marxism, MIA provides an extensive archive of articles about communism as well as biographies of noted Communists. By following the "Subjects" link, students can find essays on women and Marxism, the art and literature of the Communist age, and the current status of the Communist movement.

Reagan (www.pbs.org/wgbh/americanexperience/films/reagan). The companion website to the 1998 PBS film *Reagan* features a video titled *The Soviet Threat*, in which historians and former Soviet officials comment on President Ronald Reagan's attitude toward communism and the Soviet Union. The site also includes an audio interview with Mikhail Gorbachev, the last president of the Soviet Union.

Periodicals

Ed Adamczyk, "Flashback: Reagan Jokes About Bombing Soviet Union, 30 Years Ago," UPI, August 11, 2011. www.upi.com/Top_News/World-News/2014/08/11/Flashback-Reagan-jokes-about-bombing-Soviet-Union-30-years-ago/7591407784065.

Mark Adomanis, "What Is the Russian Middle Class? Probably Not What You Think," *Forbes*, September 10, 2012. www.forbes.com/sites/markadomanis/2012/09/10/what-is-the-russian-middle-class-probably-not-what-you-think.

Douglas Birch, "The USSR and US Came Closer to Nuclear War than We Thought," *Atlantic*, May 28, 2013. www.theatlantic.com/international/archive/2013/05/the-ussr-and-us-came-closer-to-nuclear-war-than-we-thought/276290.

Tom de Castella, "How Did We Forget About Mutually Assured Destruction?," BBC News, February 15, 2012. www.bbc.com/news/magazine-17026538.

Economist, "Stubborn Facts on the Ground: Ethnic Differences in Kyrgyzstan," April 20, 2013.